FIG. 1. Caricature, dated 1826, by an unknown artist. Courtesy of Yale Medical Library.

TRANSACTIONS OF THE
AMERICAN PHILOSOPHICAL SOCIETY
HELD AT PHILADELPHIA
FOR PROMOTING USEFUL KNOWLEDGE

VOLUME 68, PART 1 · 1978

Crowner's Quest

THOMAS ROGERS FORBES
PROFESSOR OF ANATOMY, YALE UNIVERSITY SCHOOL OF MEDICINE

THE AMERICAN PHILOSOPHICAL SOCIETY
INDEPENDENCE SQUARE: PHILADELPHIA
January 1978

For my friends the Archivists

Library of Congress Catalog Card Number 77-91655
International Standard Book Number 0-87169-681-9
US ISSN 0065-9746

FOREWORD

It is ten years since I was appointed Her Majesty's Coroner to the City of London, and during that time I have naturally interested myself in the history of my office, as well as in the day to day running of a modern coroner's jurisdiction.

In all the civilized countries of the world some form of investigation is undertaken in cases of sudden, unexpected, unexplained, unnatural, or violent death.

In England and Wales the investigation of all deaths that fall into the above categories is the responsibility of a judicial officer, the Coroner, who since the Coroner's Amendment Act of 1926 has been an appointed officer, qualified in medicine or in law.

The early history of the office reaches back through the years to the Articles of the Eyre, issued by Hubert Walter the Justiciar in 1194. There can be very little doubt that there was some machinery in being for the investigation of sudden death even before that date, for the Lex Murdrum and the Presentment of Englishery were essential parts of inquest law from the days of William the Conqueror until 1340.

In our modern and sophisticated society the words of Goldsmith in his *Elegy On Mrs. Mary Blaize*: "The doctor found when she was dead her last disorder mortal" are no longer sufficient to explain away a sudden death, even if the cause is thought to be natural.

The coroner of today, in England and Wales, owes a duty to the community to investigate every sudden, unexpected, unexplained, and unnatural death so that:

Accurate statistics of natural disease deaths can be prepared, with the associated development of preventative medicine.

Accidental deaths, associated with dangerous practices and design in such matters as transportation, industry, building, medication, and even medical practice can be exposed and corrected.

Unsuspected homicide can be discovered.

The lives and safety of persons deprived of their liberty by the state can be protected.

In short, the modern coroner has the duty so aptly expressed by the Coroner's Association of Ontario in their motto: "To Speak for the Dead, to Protect the Living."

Professor Thomas Forbes, in this overlook of London coroners' inquests for the years 1788–1829, reveals the gradual development of the system towards the modern ideal in the jurisdiction of the City of London and Southwark.

The period under review is really the nadir of the coroner's system in England and Wales, for it is the period of the unqualified coroner; of open hostility between the coroners and the justices of the peace; of lack of regulation in the disposal of a dead body; of lack of provision for the payment of medical witnesses at inquest. Some of these matters were put right by statute, in that in 1836 provision was made for the payment of medical witnesses at inquest, and as a result post-mortem examination and expert testimony became more common. In the same year regulations for the disposal of the dead were introduced in the Births and Deaths Registration Act. The hostility between the coroners and the justices continued, with the justices frustrating the coroners' attempts to hold proper enquiry into non-homicidal deaths, until the County Coroners Act of 1860 finally freed the coroners from the influence of the justices and established a salary system of payment for the coroners.

In his book Professor Forbes has found much that is fascinating to me as the present holder of the office in the City of London, and therefore the successor to such men as Thomas Beach, Thomas Shelton, and William Payne. Indeed I noticed a striking similarity between myself and Thomas Shelton in that my handwriting also varies from "the easily readable to the indecipherable."

The causes of death present a very interesting comparison with today's findings, notably the vast reduction in deaths from alcoholism and drowning and the reduction in the total numbers of deaths in young children and from homicide; the changing pattern of suicide; and the persistence of building-site accidents.

The abolition of the deodand has prevented me from assessing the value of the last Rolls Royce car involved in a fatal accident in the City and confiscating it for the Crown, and I have not as yet had the opportunity to seize a sturgeon (the Royal Fish) in the River Thames but this may yet arise as the pollution of London's river comes under control.

I found that this book provided me with a well researched and easily readable vignette of the coroner's activities in the jurisdiction of the City of London and Southwark through a period of history which has up to now been poorly chronicled. It has provided valuable comparisons between the present office and those of the past, and has whetted my appetite for further research into the historical background of my own jurisdiction.

It should provide valuable background reading for all involved or just merely interested in the development of systems of sudden death investigation, be they historians, medicolegists, lawyers, medical examiners, or coroners, the world over.

January 1976

David M. Paul
Her Majesty's Coroner
The City of London

PREFACE

Death touches us all. When the result of accident or violence, it stirs a special concern; such an end to life ought to be avoidable.[1] Fatal disease, by definition, moves inexorably toward its victim; society finds itself powerless to change his destiny. But a traffic accident, a drowning, a suicide or homicide we recognize as a tragedy that could have been prevented if someone had realized the threat to life and had moved in time.

To the concern of the observer is added that of society, which can never wholly ignore the avoidable, unnatural death of one of its members, particularly if that death may have been due to foul play. The roots of society's concern are numerous and tangled. Part of this concern is disclosed in a more or less formal effort to discover how and why the tragedy occurred. Who or what is responsible? Even if it is only suspected that death may have been violent or accidental, an investigation is or should be undertaken. The investigators now usually include the policeman, the coroner, and the pathologist. Information is sought from witnesses, from evidence, and from the dead body itself. When the facts seem to justify further action, they are passed on to the judiciary. Thus does society attempt, with whatever success, both to satisfy its curiosity as to the causes of a violent death and to prevent its repetition. The first effort usually succeeds; the second too often does not.

We shall be concerned with the operation and results of one part of this investigative system, the coroner's inquest. The surviving records of 6,351 inquests conducted by the coroners for the City of London and Southwark from 1788, when the existing series of papers began, to 1829, when my study ended, provide the basis for the present analysis. Curiously enough, these fascinating documents, in spite of their importance, appear never to have been reviewed. Indeed, while much is known about the medieval coroner and his work,[2] published information on the content of coroners' inquisitions in England from the end of Elizabeth's reign until at least the 1840's is remarkably scanty.[3] In addition to one report of my own,[4] I have found only Oakley's study of a Yorkshire death in 1676,[5] Bailey's review of 60 cases from 1746 to 1789 in the Manor of Prescot,[6] and Hair's analysis of 1,907 deaths investigated at inquests in Shropshire in 1780–1809.[7] The eighteenth- and nineteenth-century inquests comprising the present series give us facts regarding deaths from accidents on the streets, in homes, and at work, certain deaths from illness, deaths under suspicious or uncertain circumstances, and deaths from deliberate violence. The records make clear for the first time the evolution in England of regular postmortem examinations for medicolegal purposes and shed light on the operation of the inquest system. We see some of the effects of child labor, of the persistence of harsh conditions of employment, and of the substitution of machines for handwork as the Industrial Revolution developed.

The unpublished documents used in the present study are preserved in the Records Office of the Corporation of London. For access to them, for information on London prisons, and for sagacious and unstinting assistance with many questions my best thanks are offered to Miss Betty R. Masters, B.A., F.S.A., Deputy Keeper of the Records, and her staff. I am also indebted to Miss Masters for reading part of this book in manuscript and offering important suggestions. Albert E. J. Hollaender, Ph.D., F.S.A., F.R.Hist.S., former Keeper of Manuscripts, Guildhall Library, first directed me to the coroners' inquisitions, encouraged my labors, and shared his profound scholarship. Professors George Rosen and Colin White of the Yale University School of Medicine generously read the manuscript and gave wise advice and assistance. Any errors are my own.

The research for this publication was supported in part by NIH grant LM01538 from the National Library of Medicine.

T.R.F.

New Haven, Connecticut
October 1975

[1] I shall use the term *accident* rather than the more restrictive *misadventure*, a word that in any case does not appear in the present series of inquests.

[2] See, for example, R. F. Hunnisett, *The Medieval Coroner* (Cambridge, 1961).

[3] *Inquisition* refers both to certain types of investigation, including an inquest, held before a jury and to the official document reporting the finding of that jury. I shall use *inquisition* in the latter sense.

[4] T. R. Forbes, "London Coroners' Inquests for 1590," *Jour. History Med. Allied Sci.* **28** (1973): pp. 376–386.

[5] A. F. Oakley, "Reresby and the Moor," *History Med.* **3** (1971): pp 27–29.

[6] F. A. Bailey, "Coroners' Inquests Held in the Manor of Prescot, 1746–89," *Trans. Histor. Soc. Lancashire and Cheshire* **86** (1934): pp. 21–39.

[7] P. E. H. Hair, "Accidental Death and Suicide in Shropshire, 1780–1809," *Trans. Shropshire Archaeol. Soc.* **59** (1969): pp. 63–75.

CROWNER'S QUEST

Thomas Rogers Forbes

CONTENTS

I. THE CORONER AND THE INQUEST

The coronership was established in England in September, 1194.[1] Whether an equivalent office existed earlier is a problem not yet satisfactorily resolved. Elected by the freeholders of the county, the coroner (*coronarius* or, as in Magna Carta, *coronator*) retained his position for life if he satisfied the requirement for good behavior. Four coroners were elected for each county and were obliged to live there. Upon election a coroner swore an oath of office before the sheriff.

The coronership as established provided a mechanism both for administering justice and for insuring that the royal interest in certain sources of revenue was recorded, protected, and exploited. The coroner was the *custos placitorum coronae*, the guardian of the pleas of the crown; as such, his judicial obligation seems to have been quite secondary to his financial responsibility. He pursued revenues for the crown in several quarters. Convicted felons, for example, in addition to suffering imprisonment, maiming, loss of life, or other punishment forfeited to the king their goods and chattels. It was up to the coroner to determine what these were and how much they were worth. Again, in the Middle Ages the commission of a crime was regarded in part as representing a failure of the community to maintain law and order. Heavy fines or amercements were laid on the men in the town, village, or rural area held responsible. Here also the coroner was involved, since the fines went to the king.

In the beginning the coroner was not paid, a serious defect in the system. Corruption was the inevitable result. When the coronership was established, it had been specified that three knights and one clerk be elected from each county. It may have been hoped that a knight's wealth would set him above financial temptation. If he were convicted of accepting bribes or of embezzlement, his possessions could be seized. But dishonesty spread. Supervision of the coroners was insufficient, and punishments were not heavy enough to be effective. The status of the office sank further as responsible individuals refused to accept a position that was both time-consuming and lacking in lawful remuneration. Extortion became widespread, the coroners and their clerks demanding payment before calling inquests.

In 1487 an act (3 Henry VII, c. 2) was passed permitting the coroner a fee of one mark for each inquest into a homicide plus fourpence from the goods and chattels of the guilty man. The coroner was subject to a severe fine when he failed to hold an inquest, but the lack of a fee in a case of death by accident naturally tempted him not to bother with an

[1] The history of the English coroner's office and of its theoretical and actual functions during the twelfth through the eighteenth centuries has been told before. I offer here a summary, drawn chiefly from Norman Brodrick *et al.*, *Report of the Committee on Death Certification and Coroners* (London, 1971), pp. x, 9, 107–114, 119; Anthony Fitzherbert, *The New Booke of Justices of Peace* (London, 1545, no pagination); Charles Gross, ed., "Select Cases from the Coroners' Rolls A.D. 1265–1413 with a Brief Account of the Office of Coroner," *Selden Soc. Publ.* (London, 1896) **9**: pp. xiv–xv, xx, xxiv–xxvi; J. D. J. Havard, *The Detection of Secret Homicide* (London, 1960), pp. 1–11, 38, 42–45; R. F. Hunnisett, "Bedfordshire Coroners' Rolls," *Publ. Bedfordshire Histor. Record Soc.* **41** (1961): pp. v–vii, ix; *ibid.*, *The Medieval Coroner*, pp. 1–14; I. L. Langbein, "The Jury of Presentment and the Coroner," *Columbia Law Rev.* **33** (1933): pp. 1329–1365; D. I. Macht, "The Ancient Office of Coroner," *Johns Hopkins Hosp. Bull.* **24** (1913): pp. 148–153; A. K. Mant, "Official Medico-legal Investigation under the Coroner's System in London, England," *Medico-Legal. Bull.* **20** (1971): pp. 1–8, No. 223; H. H. Pilling, "Social Change and the Coronership," *Med. Sci. Law* **10** (1970): 238–243; W. B. Purchase and H. W. Wollaston, *Jervis on the Office and Duties of Coroner* (London, 1957), pp. 23–25; E. D. Shapiro and Anthony Davis, "Law and Pathology through the Ages. The Coroner and His Descendants—Legitimate and Illegitimate," *N.Y. State Jour. Med.* **72** (1972): pp. 805–809; J. F. Stephen, *A History of the Criminal Law of England* (London, 1883) **1**: pp. 216–219; E. Umfreville, *Lex coronatoria* (London, 1761), pp. lix, 26. F. J. Waldo, "The Ancient Office of Coroner," *Trans. Med.-Legal Soc. (London)* **8** (1911): pp. 101–133; R. H. Wellington, *The King's Coroner* (London, 1905), pp. 1, 3, 69–70; W. W. Westcott, "A Note upon Deodands," *Trans. Med.-Leg. Soc. (London)* **10** (1910): pp. 91–97; John Wilkinson, *A treatise . . . concerning the office and authorities of coroners and sheriffs* (London, 1651), pp. 1–4.

investigation. In 1509 another act (1 Hen. VIII, c. 7) recited the evil that had developed.

> If any person hath happened to be slain by misadventure and not by no man's hand that they [the coroners] will not enquire upon the view of the body so by misadventure slain except they have for their labour thirteen shillings and fourpence, which is contrary to the Common Law . . .; whereby great inconvenience doth daily grow to the King's Subjects, forasmuch as often-times the person that is so by misadventure slain lieth long above the ground unburied, to the great annoyance of the King's liege people.

The act directed the coroner to investigate an accidental death without demanding a fee. It was ordered

> that upon a request made to a Coroner to come and inquire upon the view of any person slain drowned or otherwise dead by misadventure, the said Coroner diligently do his office upon the view of the body of every such person or persons without anything [i.e., a payment] taking.

A fine of 40*s*. was to be imposed for each violation of the act. The necessity for its passage implies continuing neglect on the part of the coroner.

Legislation attempting to rectify the decay of the coroner's office did not come for almost two and a half centuries. In 1751 an act (25 George II, c. 29) was passed which was intended to improve the remuneration of the coroner by authorizing him to receive for each inquest 20*s*. as a fee plus 9*d*. for each mile he traveled. Under this law, in addition, extortion, neglect of duty, or misdemeanor in office were grounds for the coroner's removal. However, the success of the new legislation was seriously interfered with by the standing quarrel between the coroners and the justices of the peace. The latter, who had long since assumed responsibility for the maintenance of local law and order, took the position that the coroner should not conduct inquests in cases of sudden death unless there clearly had been violence. The coroners claimed jurisdiction in all instances of sudden and unexplained death, whether violent or not. The justices enforced their views by withholding coroners' fees and even by attempting to prevent word of sudden deaths reaching the coroners. The office continued in a state of disrespect and ineffectiveness.

During the Middle Ages the duties of the coroner were in theory and in the law books numerous but in fact, as revealed by the coroners' records of their activities, were fewer than is generally believed.[2] The actual duties included the appraisal and recording of goods and chattels of persons committing homicide and suicide,[3] outlaws, confessed felons, and abjurors of the realm.[4] In relatively few cases was the coroner concerned with determining the value of shipwrecks, "royal fishes,"[5] and treasure trove[6] owed to the crown. By far his most important and frequent duty was to hold inquests upon dead bodies, specifically, the bodies of persons who had died from other than natural causes, or in prison, or suddenly, or in circumstances which appeared or were reported to be suspicious.

In the Middle Ages, when such a body was found, the coroner was supposed to be summoned by the "first finder." If the coroner was not called, the township in which the death occurred could be subject to a fine. However, since it was well known that the "finder" himself might be amerced if he did not follow the correct procedure, it is said that many individuals failed to report the discovery of bodies. If a corpse was buried instead of being guarded until the coroner arrived, it had to be exhumed and those responsible for the premature burial were fined. If some resourceful individuals succeeded in transporting a body to another locality, hoping thereby to avoid trouble, again a law was broken and amercements were laid on the guilty. No doubt these illegal maneuvers sometimes succeeded; the records tell us only of the failures.

For the inquest a jury, usually of twelve to sixteen men, had to be assembled by the sheriff or bailiff. In the thirteenth century the jury was drawn from the township in which the body had been found and from three adjoining townships. After the jurors had assembled they were sworn in by the coroner, promising to speak the truth. Then all viewed the naked body, looking for external signs—bruises, wounds, etc.—of death from other than natural causes. The dimensions of any wound were measured and noted. If a weapon or weapons were responsible, they were preserved and described. Here could arise a knotty problem that troubles coroners and their juries to this day: was death due to a natural cause or to an injury received earlier? As we shall see, this can be a most perplexing question.

Anthony Fitzherbert's *The New Booke of Justices of Peace*, published in 1545, includes instructions for the coroner.[7] He and the jurors were to

> view the body, and the woundes, and the strokes, and immediatly after suche viewe had the bodye shalbe buryed. And yf the Coroner fynde the bodye buried before his comminge, he shall recorde the same, nevertheles he shall not omitte to digge up the body. . . .
>
> And when the inquest is sworne ye Coroner must inquire if ye person were slayne by felony, or by misadventure, & whether ye felony were done within a house, or without, & all ye circumstance. And after it shalbe enquired who were presente at the dede, and who be coulpable of the ayde, force, commandement, consent, or receite of suche felonies wittingly.

---

[2] Hunnisett, *The Medieval Coroner*, pp. 4–9.

[3] A person who had committed a homicide, like he who was found guilty of *felo de se*, was adjudged a felon and his property was therefore forfeit. Forfeiture of the goods of a convicted felon was not abolished until 1870 (33 and 34 Vict., c. 23) (Waldo, p. 122).

[4] Unless he had been judged guilty of sacrilege or treason, a felon who had found sanctuary could claim immunity by leaving the realm after taking an oath or swearing never to return except with royal permission.

[5] Whales, sturgeons, and porpoises when cast ashore or captured in territorial waters belonged to the king regardless of who had found or caught them.

[6] Money, bullion, etc. found in the earth and of unknown ownership became the property of the crown.

[7] Fitzherbert, no pagination.

In the Middle Ages and later, deaths in prison were not uncommon. In that crowded and unsanitary environment, infectious diseases were easily spread. Jail fever (typhus) took a particularly heavy toll among those imprisoned, their keepers, and persons attending court, not excepting the judge himself. Neglect, bad food, starvation, and mistreatment were sometimes lethal. So it was important that an inquest be held when a prisoner died, whether from natural causes or otherwise. However, while the intention may have been good, the coroner's jury nearly always decided that death in prison was from natural causes *ex visitatione divina*, "by the visitation of God".[8] We shall return to this topic.

The coroner's jurisdiction over deaths at sea was not so clearly defined. Fitzherbert wrote in the sixteenth century:[9]

> The coroner shall enquire of the death of men slaine, or drowned in the armes, or creekes of the see where the lande may be sene of eyther syde. But nowe by the statute made . . . the admyral hath no iurisdiccyon, but onely upon the hyghe see, whereby it apperyth that the Coroner hathe iurysdyccion there to enquyre of mannes death.

Another sometimes puzzling problem was the animate (but nonhuman) or inanimate object that caused an accidental death. In law, *omnia quae movent ad mortem, deodanda sunt*, all things moving to a death are deodands. The term derived from the ancient idea that the object responsible for the death had sinned and that the sin could be expiated by giving the object or its equivalent value to the Church.[10] Hence *deodandum*, something that should be given to God. However, by the end of the twelfth century the deodand or a sum equivalent in value usually went to the crown.[11] The coroner was expected to determine the ownership of the deodand, and the coroner's jury was obliged to establish its value. In the aggregate, deodands must have been a significant source of revenue to the crown, even though in London they somehow found their way into the treasury of the City instead of the king.

Naturally the deodand system engendered a variety of problems over the centuries. If, for example, a sailor fell into the Thames between a wherry and a ship and was crushed, which vessel was the deodand? When the sail of a windmill struck and killed a woman, should the sail or the entire mill be forfeit? In addition, it was not unusual for a sympathetic coroner's jury to spare a fellow townsman by deliberately underestimating the value of his deodand. Most deodands are said to have been of relatively small value before the advent of the Machine Age. However, when factories, ships, and trains with their steam-powered machinery came into use, forfeitures of deodands could be ruinous, as in a case in 1838 when a jury set a value of £1,500 on the boiler of a ship's steam engine that exploded.[12] A spate of complicated law suits resulted from such situations. Nevertheless, deodands were not abolished until August 18, 1846 (9 & 10 Vict., cap. 62).[11]

Since the coroner was obliged to keep records of the inquests he conducted on dead bodies, in effect he was unknowingly assembling raw data that would eventually contribute to the yet unborn science of vital statistics. But actual study of the causes of death developed very slowly. The story may be said to begin with the parish registers, books in which the clerk or curate recorded baptisms, marriages, and burials. From this information evolved as early as 1519 the Bills of Mortality.[13] These were official periodic lists for London and its vicinity giving, parish by parish, the numbers of deaths and, later, also of births. Angus[14] concluded that "to the plague the public of London owed their bills of christenings and deaths." Certainly the recording of fatalities from this disease was a conspicuous feature of the weekly Bills. By 1536, a plague year, the parish clerks were instructed to submit to the Lord Mayor of London written weekly lists of the names of the sick and dead. The collection and recording of such information became the responsibility of the Parish Clerks' Company toward the middle of the sixteenth century, and by the end of that century printed weekly and yearly Bills of Mortality were appearing.[13]

The science of vital statistics was founded by John Graunt (1620–1674), London haberdasher and freeman of the Drapers' Company. His *Natural and Political Observations on the Bills of Mortality*,[15] first published in 1662, was a compilation and interpretation of their data. While at first, as Graunt indicates, the only specific cause of death that was recorded was plague, by 1629 "an account of the diseases and casualties, whereof any died, together with the distinction of males and females" was being regularly reported. The Bill for 1632 lists 9,535 burials. Among them were 1 death for "Bit with a made dog," 5 "Burnt and scalded," 6 "Dead in the street, and starved," 4 "Drowned," 38 "Executed and prest to death," 6 "Killed by several accidents," 15 "Made away themselves," 7 "Murthered," 7 "Overlaid, and starved at nurse," and 62 "Suddenly."

Then Graunt examines 229,250 deaths in the twenty years 1629–1636 and 1647–1658. (He does not explain why these years were chosen.) In tables he lists the numbers of deaths from "the more formidable and notorious diseases" and from "casualties." The latter

[8] Forbes, "London Coroner's Inquests for 1590."

[9] Fitzherbert, no pagination.

[10] E. P. Evans, *The Criminal Prosecution and Capital Punishment of Animals* (New York, 1906); W. W. Hyde, "The Prosecution and Punishment of Animals and Lifeless things in the Middle Ages and Modern Times," *Univ. Penna. Law Review* **64** (1916): pp. 696–730.

[11] Bailey, "Coroners' Inquests Held in the Manor of Prescot, 1746–89" (n. 1): "Bedfordshire Coroners' Rolls," p. ix; *The Medieval Coroner*, p. 32; Umfreville, *Lex coronatoria*, p. 97 *et seq.*; Waldo, p. 118; Wellington, pp. 14–18; Westcott; Wilkinson, pp. 9, 23.

[12] (N. 1), Westcott, p. 93.

[13] T. R. Forbes, *Chronicle from Aldgate* (New Haven, 1971), pp. 46–49, 52–56.

[14] John Angus, "Old and New Bills of Mortality . . . ," *Jour. Statist. Soc. London* **17** (1854): pp. 117–142.

[15] John Graunt, *Natural and Political Observations* (London, 1759), pp. 5–6, 10, 43.

list probably represents the earliest separate tabulation of deaths by accident and violence in London.

TABLE OF CASUALTIES

Bleeding	69
Burnt and scalded	125
Drowned	829
Excessive drinking	2
Frighted	22
Grief	279
Hanged themselves	222
Killed by several accidents	1021
Murdered	86
Poisoned	14
Smothered	26
Shot	7
Starved	51
Vomiting	136

We would not consider some of the above to be "casualties," nor would we include, as Graunt does, 529 "Overlaid and starved" infants in a separate list of "notorious diseases."

His work suffered from several deficiencies, some of them unavoidable because certain data were not available to him[16] and some because of defects in the reporting of the causes of death. When an individual died, the parish clerk was notified, the church bell was tolled, and one or two "searchers" were sent by the clerk to examine the body of the deceased.[17] London records refer to searchers, persons originally employed to examine or "view" cadavers for signs of plague, as early as 1578. Later on the searchers were supposed to report all causes of death. Because the pay was poor, impoverished old women usually were the only candidates for this unpleasant and sometimes dangerous job, a sad footnote to the history of social economics. The "antient matrons" were sworn to carry out their duties promptly, carefully, and honestly, but there is abundant evidence, including some from Graunt, that the opposite was often true. The searchers depended on what they saw and on what they learned from observers in arriving at the cause of death. The poverty-stricken women could be bribed to make false reports, as in concealing a case of plague so that the family of the deceased could escape quarantine. If a searcher was illiterate, she had to persuade some one to write her report for her. There were many complaints about the system, but it continued into the nineteenth century, and there can be little doubt that most of the information on causes of death in the Bills of Mortality derived from the searchers.

After Graunt, there appeared a number of other analyses of the Bills of Mortality and of related information.[18] But the machinery to accumulate reliable and complete statistics on death still was lacking. Progress was achieved in 1836 with the passage of the Births and Deaths Registration Act, which provided for the registration of deaths in England and Wales.[19] The first of the invaluable reports of the Registrars General appeared in 1839, covering the year ending June 30, 1838. The *Sixth Annual Report* included a detailed analysis of accidental and violent deaths in London in 1840, the first such English study to be published.[20] The Bills of Mortality, which had continued regularly since 1603, were superseded and came to an end in 1842.

Passage of the Births and Deaths Registration Act in effect introduced a measure of reform into the operations of the coroners. The act provided for local and district registrars. Several categories of deaths, including those of children who had not been baptized, still did not require registration. However, the reporting of most deaths was regularized. An important result was that it became much more difficult to conceal homicides.

II. INQUESTS IN 1788–1829

Thomas Beach, coroner of the City of London and the Borough of Southwark, died early in the summer of 1788. On July 24, Thomas Shelton, his assistant for the preceding seven years, petitioned the Lord Mayor, Aldermen, and Commons of the City of London for election as Beach's successor.[1] Shelton was an attorney, not a medical man. He argued that the coroner's office was "a branch of the criminal law" and that he was qualified by both training and experience. Shelton was duly elected to hold office and to receive all fees and profits pertaining to it. He served continuously thereafter, his final official appearance taking place two days before his death on July 10, 1829. During his forty-one years as the only Coroner of the City and Southwark, Shelton conducted more than six thousand inquests.[2] A bachelor and reputedly wealthy, he was highly respected and held several Corporation appointments.[3]

On July 14 the Common Council appointed William Lewis Newman, the City's solicitor, to serve temporarily in Shelton's place. A report submitted to

[16] J. H. Cassedy, "Introduction," in: *Mortality in Preindustrial Times* (Westmead, Farnborough, Hants, 1973), n.p.

[17] T. R. Forbes, "The Searchers," *Bull. N.Y. Acad. Med.*, second ser., **50** (1974): pp. 1031–1038.

[18] Sir William Petty, *Essay on Political Arithmetic* (1683, London); Thomas Short, *New Observations . . . on City, Town, and Country Bills of Mortality* (London, 1750); [T. Birch, ed.], *A Collection of the Yearly Bills of Mortality* (London, 1759); J. Marshall, *Mortality of the Metropolis* (London, 1832); J. C. Platt, "Bills of Mortality," in: Charles Knight, ed., *London* (London, 1844) **6**: pp. 225–240; J. R. McCulloch, *A Descriptive and Statistical Account of the British Empire* (London, 1854) **2**: pp. 565–569; William Farr, *Vital Statistics* (London, 1885).

[19] 6 and 7 Will. IV, c. 86; (n. 1), Havard, pp. 44–48.

[20] *Sixth Annual Report* of the Registrar General (London, 1845), pp. 210–211, 232–241, 252–266. However, as late as 1881 Walford was to deplore the lack of comprehensive studies of such deaths ("On the Number of Deaths from Accident, Negligence, Violence, and Misadventure in the United Kingdom and Some Other Countries," *Jour. Statist. Soc.* **44**: pp. 444–527).

[1] "Journal of the Common Council of the City of London," Corporation of London Records Office, **71**, July 24, 1788.

[2] All inquisitions, an unknown number, for 1800 are missing.

[3] *Minutes of the Common Council* (London), July 14, 1829, p. 75. "Thomas Shelton, Esq.," *Gentleman's Mag.* **99**, 2 (1829): p. 89.

the Council on August 6, 1829, implicitly recognizing the problem created by Shelton's demise, urged that a legal officer of the Corporation be empowered to serve in the place of the coroner when the latter was prevented by illness or otherwise from doing so.[4] The report stated that the duties of the office were

> to issue precepts for summoning juries to attend on inquests to be taken on view of all persons who die in prisons within the city and borough, and on all persons who come to their deaths by violence or otherwise, except by natural disease or infirmity.
>
> To attend and view the body and examine and take the depositions of witnesses, to record the verdicts, draw up the inquisitions, and grant warrants to bury; and in cases of culpable homicide to commit to prison or issue warrants against the offenders, and to bind over by recognizance the witnesses to attend and prosecute and give evidence.
>
> To attend the trials of such inquisitions as are returned to the Sessions or Assizes against persons for murder or manslaughter.
>
> To execute all writs against the Sheriffs, and all writs in cases wherein the Sheriffs are parties or are interested.

The report urged that the coroner should have a legal education. It added that Shelton had stated that his income from the coronership had been £631.3.10 in 1820, £731.12.0 in 1821, and £891.6.0 in 1822, more than half of this coming from the execution of writs. The Committee recommended that in the future the coroner should in addition to such emoluments receive a guinea for each inquest he conducted but not be allowed any other compensation.[5] In 1850 a successful barrister, by comparison, might have had an income of £5,000 a year.[6]

At the Common Council meeting on September 9, 1829, John Gordon Smith, M.D., professor of medical jurisprudence at the University of London, petitioned for appointment to the coronership of the City and Southwark.[7] His position and experience should have made him well qualified. Nevertheless he was not elected, and at a meeting on September 24 a committee examining the office expressed the opinion that

> it will not be expedient for this court to confine the qualifications of the Candidates for the Office of Coroner, either to the Legal, Medical, or any particular profession, but that any Gentleman of experience, respectable Character, and liberal Education, is duly qualified to fill that Office.

Smith tried again on October 22, this time asking to be made an associate of the coroner so that the professor could supply "that assistance, which Medical Science only can impart."[8] But his petition was tabled. At the same meeting five candidates for coroner were voted on. The office went to William Payne, "Citizen and Gun-Maker" but qualified neither in medicine nor law. Apparently the Council preferred a member of one of the craft guilds. Payne conducted his first inquest on October 26, 1829.

There are two gaps in the 1788–1829 series of inquisitions. As already mentioned, all inquisitions are missing for the year 1800. In addition, there are only three inquisitions for July, 1829, presumably because of Shelton's fatal illness and the lack of a substitute coroner, none for August and September, and three at the end of October, after William Payne had taken office. Inquisitions appear in their normal numbers in November and December.

At the Common Council meeting on September 9 the inhabitants of Southwark had requested their own coroner.[7] Apparently nothing came of this, but the residents of this great borough had a point. Its population in 1821 was 85,905, as compared to a population in that year for the City, including the parishes without the walls, of 125,434.[9]

Table 1 indicates the geographic and institutional distribution of the 6,351 inquests in our series. Inquests known to have been on the bodies of prisoners and of hospital patients are listed separately and are not included in the totals for those City wards and Southwark parishes in which the prisons and hospitals were located, even though inquests on prisoners were often held in the parish church. Inquests on prisoners dying in Newgate, for example, were usually conducted in Christ Church (Ward of Farringdon Within) or St. Sepulchre (Ward of Farringdon Without), both contiguous to the prison. Similarly, St. Thomas's Parish in Southwark included Guy's and the old St. Thomas's Hospitals and a small additional area. To have counted the inquests on hospital patients and prisoners with those on residents of the parish would be misleading. In addition, the numbers of deaths recorded for the various prisons do not tell the whole story. When a prison was rebuilt, its name was often carried to the new site. This occurred in 1791, when prisoners from both Wood Street and Poultry Compters were moved to the new prison in Giltspur Street. Wood Street and Poultry Compters continued to exist as separate sections of the prison. Ludgate Prison was demolished in 1761, the prisoners being moved first to a part of the London Workhouse in Bishopsgate Street and then, in 1795, to still another section of the Giltspur Street Compter. White Cross Street Prison for debtors was not opened until 1817.

Variations in the numbers of inquests also reflect, of course, the great differences in the size of wards and parishes and in the numbers of their inhabitants. It should be noted that in the case of accidental deaths in or on the Thames, of which there were many, the victims were brought ashore to the nearest parish and the inquests were held there, thus adding some extraparochial deaths to the totals for the parishes along

---

[4] *Report of the Officers and Clerk's Committee on the Office of Coroner of London and Southwark Presented to Common Council August 6, 1829* (1829, London), pp. 4–5.

[5] *Ibid.*, p. 4.

[6] John Burnett, *A History of the Cost of Living* (Harmondsworth, Middlesex, 1969), p. 233.

[7] (N. 2), p. 83.

[8] *Ibid.*, p. 98.

[9] John Hogg, *London As It Is* (1837, London), pp. 196–198.

TABLE 1

GEOGRAPHICAL AND INSTITUTIONAL DISTRIBUTIONS OF INQUESTS

City Wards		
Aldersgate Within	64	
Aldgate	61	
Bassishaw	6	
Billingsgate	177	
Bishopsgate	193	
Bread Street	21	
Bridge	59	
Broad Street	46	
Candlewick	20	
Castle Baynard	78	
Cheap	40	
Coleman Street	57	
Cordwainer	22	
Cornhill	12	
Cripplegate	159	
Dowgate	82	
Farringdon Within	113	
Farringdon Without	713	
Langbourn	40	
Lime Street	14	
Portsoken	92	
Queenhithe	79	
Tower	219	
Vintry	41	
Walbrook	16	
		2424
Southwark Parishes		
St. George the Martyr	247	
St. John	387	
St. Olave	295	
St. Saviour	38	
St. Thomas	179	
		1146
City Prisons		
Bridewell	98	
Fleet	281	
Ludgate	15	
Newgate	539	
Poultry, Wood St., and Giltspur St. Compters	172	
White Cross	98	
		1203
Southwark Prisons		
Borough Compter	1	
Bridewell	16	
County ("New Gaol")	43	
		60
City Hospitals		
Bethlem	2	
St. Bartholomew's	726	
		728
Southwark Hospitals		
Guy's	293	
St. Thomas's	497	
		790
		6351

the river. Inquests were held in, or as close as possible to, the parish where death actually occurred. Of course the victim might have been injured or been suddenly taken ill in another parish, might be a resident of a different parish, and so on.

An inquest required a public room large enough to accommodate the coroner, a clerk, jurymen, witnesses, parish officials, and whatever spectators were admitted. The actual site was only infrequently identified in the records, particularly in the earlier years, but probably it was often the vestry room of a church or a hall in a workhouse. Later on many inquests were held in hospitals as more and more persons died there,[10] and beginning in 1824 there is evidence that on occasion a public house provided the necessary place of assembly.

I found no instances of an inquest when the body was missing, as when a drowning had been observed but the body was not recovered. Indeed, the inquisition always spoke of the jurors' "view of the Body," a procedure required by law.

When the coroner learned of a death that required an inquest, he sent to the beadle and constables of the appropriate parish a warrant for them to assemble jurors. Until May, 1792, this document was handwritten, but thereafter the coroner used a printed form in which the necessary details were inserted. A typical warrant for 1790 read as follows.

> To the Beadles and Constables of the Parish of Christ Church in the Ward of Farringdon within London.
>
> To wit, By virtue of my Office these are in his Majesty's Name to charge and command you that on sight hereof you Summon and Warn twenty four good and Sufficient men of your Parish and Ward personally to be and appear before me on Wednesday the Sixth Day of January inst. at Nine of the Clock in the Morning of the same day as this at His Majesty's Gaol of Newgate situate in the Parish and Ward aforesaid.
>
> Then and there to do and execute all such things that shall be given them in charge and to inquire on the behalf of our Sovereign Lord the King touching the death of Thomas Sneard and for your so doing this shall be your warrant and that you attend at the time and place above mentioned to make a return of the names of those whom you have summoned and further to do and execute such other matters as shall be then and there injoined you and have you then and there this Warrant Given under my Hand and Seal this Seventh Day of January 1790.
>
> Thomas Shelton
> Coroner

A list, or tally, of the men called for jury service bore check marks against some names, presumably those of the men who actually served. Such a list was a usual component of the bundle of papers folded together and preserved after each inquest. Other components were the precept to summon the jury, the inquisition itself, and handwritten summaries of the depositions of witnesses.

For some reason, a clerk in the Parish of St. Catherine Cree, Aldgate, recorded the occupations of the members of three jury panels in 1802 and 1805.

Baker
Brandy merchant
Cabinet maker
Carpenter
Carver and gilder
Cheese monger
China man[11]
Coach maker

[10] This phenomenon will be discussed later.
[11] A dealer in, or maker of, porcelain.

Color man
Corn factor[12]
Cutler
Dyer
Fan maker
Green grocer
Grocer
Haberdasher
Hair dresser
Ham merchant
Handwareman
Hatter
Hop seller
Hosier
Iron monger
Jeweler
Linen draper
Mercer
Oil man
Optician
Painter and glazier
Pastry cook
Perfumer
Saddler
Scale maker
Shoe maker
Silver smith
Stationer
Stone mason
Tailor
Tallow chandler
Tin plate worker
Tea dealer
Turner
Victualler
Watch maker
Wine merchant
Woolen draper
Woolen dresser

One notes that, whether by intent or otherwise, the list includes no laborers, no professional men, and no members of the leisure class.

I have not found in the 1788–1829 series any documents indicating how witnesses were identified or were ordered to attend an inquest, but Edward Umfreville, senior coroner of the County of Middlesex, in 1761[13] had quoted the form for a "Summons for a Witness."

Whereas I am credibly informed you can give Evidence on Behalf of our Sovereign Lord the King, touching the death of A.B. now lying dead, in the Parish of *A*. in the said County of Middlesex; these are therefore, by Virtue of my Office, in his Majesty's Name, to charge and command you personally to be and appear before me. . . .

The summons was to be signed by the coroner.

At an inquest the coroner was primarily concerned with the circumstances of death; the medical witness, if any, with the actual medical cause of death. Of course the two questions often overlapped. The inquisition, the formal report of the inquest, signed and sealed by the coroner and the members of his jury, reported the circumstances and cause, named the deceased if possible, identified and put a price on the deodand, if there was one, named the person, if any, responsible for the death if he were known, and categorized the death as accidental, natural, etc. If a weapon was used, it was described in some detail. Beginning in April, 1807, the locations, nature, and dimensions of injuries, particularly those inflicted by weapons, were set forth.

The text of a representative inquisition in a 1789 homicide case follows.

London. An Inquisition Indented[14] taken for our Sovereign Lord the King at the parish of Saint Botolph without Aldgate in the ward of Portsoken in London aforesaid on the thirteenth day of July in the Twenty ninth Year of the Reign of our Sovereign Lord George the third by the grace of God of Great Britain France and Ireland King Defender of the faith and so forth Before Thomas Shelton Gentleman Coroner of our said Lord the King for the City of London and Borough of Southwark on view of the Body of John Edis then and there lying dead by the oath of [here follow the names of the 23 jurymen] good and lawful Men of the said City of London now here sworn and charged to Inquire for our said Lord the King when how and in what manner the said John Edis came to his Death say upon their Oath that the said John Edis on the Eleventh day of July in the Twenty ninth year aforesaid about the hour of two in the night of the same day with force and Arms at London, that is to say, at the parish and Ward aforesaid in London aforesaid the Dwelling house of one William Tyler there situate feloniously and Burglariously did break and enter with intention one Elizabeth Tyler Spinster in the peace of God and our said Lord the King and in the said Dwelling house then and there being unlawfully burglariously and feloniously to assault and her the said Elizabeth Tyler against the Will of her the said Elizabeth Tyler then and there burglariously and feloniously to Ravish and carnally know against the form of the statute in such Case made and provided and against the peace of our said Lord the King his Crown and Dignity And the Jurors aforesaid upon their Oath aforesaid do further say that William Tyler the younger then and there being in the said Dwelling house in order to prevent the said John Edis from carrying into Execution and compleating his aforesaid felonious and burglarious intention and in defence of the Chastity of the said Elizabeth Tyler Justifiably and of inevitable necessity did Attack and Assault the said John Edis and that the said William Tyler the Younger a certain pistol loaded with Gunpowder and two leaden Bullets which he the said William Tyler the younger in his right hand then and there had and held to at and against the said John Edis justifiably and of inevitable necessity did shoot off and discharge giving to him the said John Edis then and there with the leaden Bullets aforesaid shot off and discharged by force of the Gunpowder from the said pistol by him the said William Tyler the Younger as aforesaid two mortal wounds in and through the neck of him the said John Edis of which said Mortal Wounds he the said John Edis did then and there instantly die And so the Jurors aforesaid upon their Oath aforesaid do say that the said William Tyler the Younger the said John Edis in manner and by the means aforesaid Justifiably and of inevitable necessity did kill and slay In Witness whereof as well the said Coroner and the said Jurors have to this Inquisition set their hands and Seals the day Year and place first above written.

Aside from proper names and dates, the formula for each inquisition was virtually the same down to the point where the jurors "say upon their Oath" what they believed happened. Thereafter there was one formula for accidents, another for natural deaths, and so on. Similar but not identical formulas had been set forth by Umfreville in 1761[15]; no doubt the coroners exercised some discretion in this matter.

Most of the inquisitions were on paper, about 12 × 18 inches; a few were on parchment. The first printed form for an inquisition was dated June 13, 1804. Thereafter these sheets appeared intermittently,

[12] A corn merchant.

[13] Umfreville, *Lex coronatoria*, p. 511.

[14] *Indented* indicated that this document was the duplicate of another. At one time identical copies were written on the same sheet of paper and then were cut apart along an irregular line. Or copies were written on separate sheets, the two were held together, and a crooked line was cut at the top or bottom of both. Some of the inquisitions in this series had such a jagged margin.

[15] (N. 13), pp. 474–477.

but by 1809 printed inquisition forms were in regular use. The introductory formula provided blanks for insertion of names, dates, and places, and the lower part of the document contained an ample blank space in which the rest of the inquisition was written. Less admirable were occasional printed forms that were entirely free of handwritten entries except for the signatures and seals of the coroner and jury members. Presumably the coroner or his clerk had intended to fill in the necessary information at a later date. Such incomplete inquisitions were fairly common in 1807, 1808, 1815, the first half of 1823, 1824, and 1825 and occurred infrequently in 1826 and 1827. When the inquisitions were blank or missing, all my information had to be derived from the endorsement (virtually always present), depositions, and summons.

Printed inquisitions bearing not only the usual introductory formula but also standard wording indicating a verdict of natural death of a prisoner were employed. The majority of the inquisitions and depositions were in the hand of Thomas Shelton, whose writing varied from the easily readable to the almost indecipherable, presumably when haste and fatigue overcame him. Inquisitions beginning with the first, dated July 7, 1788, and continuing through 1793 bore serial numbers. No numbers were missing.

The verbal depositions of witnesses were summarized in longhand, apparently by the coroner himself. (Scraps of paper bearing preliminary notes occasionally were found.) The witness then signed or made his mark. Frequently there appeared at the bottom of a deposition, or of a series of them, the statement "Subscribed and sworn to before me . . .," the coroner's name, and perhaps the date. Statements regarding medical findings submitted by physicians were in different hands, sometimes their own.[16] By the end of the eighteenth century the majority of such statements were being submitted by dressers[17] and, occasionally, by apothecaries.

Depositions of course varied greatly. The following is a typical deposition by a prisoner in 1789.

> Thomas Brown a Prisoner in His Majesty's Gaol of Newgate maketh Oath that he hath known the deced [deceased] John Williams about Seven Months that he was also a Prisoner in the said Gaol that he hath been in the Sick Ward where Deponent attends five Months very ill with a Decline or Consumption that he continued to get worse daily until last Night when he departed this Life that he was attended by the Surgeon of the said Gaol and Dept. believes the aforesaid Complaint occasioned the deced's death.
>
> [Signed] Thomas Brown

For my analysis, as in table 1, of geographic areas involved I have used the site of the inquest. For tabulation by date, the date of the inquest was employed. Sometimes the subject of the inquest had died on that day; often death occurred a day or two earlier; infrequently the interval had been even longer, as after some drownings in the Thames. Quite often a day of the week instead of the date is specified for the time of injury and/or death, as "Wednesday last" or "Monday sennight."

Definite information as to age of the deceased and of witnesses was usually not included. The term *infant* was used for babies and children. Sometimes collateral evidence made it clear that the latter were as old as ten years. I classified individuals as adults when the context would support this (e.g., a coachman, a mason) and, more arbitrarily, classified apprentices as adults. Apprentices were supposed to be at least fourteen years old, but it is known that younger boys and girls were sometimes apprenticed illegally. When age was specified, it was usually that of a young child or of a very old person.

After the inquest the coroner issued a formal permission for burial. Two of these documents, one handwritten and one a printed form with written insertions, that were signed by Thomas Shelton are preserved in the Guildhall Library, London.[18] Obviously the requirement of such permission was a measure intended to prevent burial before the body had been viewed by the coroner and his jury.

III. DEATHS FROM OCCUPATIONAL ACCIDENTS

Accidents are always with us. Participation in a hazardous occupation increases the chance of injury or even death. Ignorance, indifference, and error also put laboring people at risk. Lack of concern for human lives, particularly those of slave laborers of antiquity, had deadly results,[1] but paid employees as well have always suffered when employers failed to recognize occupational hazards or chose to disregard them. The development of machinery and the advent of the Industrial Revolution brought new dangers.[2] Reforms in respect to dangerous working conditions developed slowly, and real improvement was not to come in England until the 1830's. It is true that the Health and Morals of Apprentices Act, introduced into the House of Commons in 1802, was intended to alleviate conditions by reducing the working day to twelve hours and enforcing the ventilation of work rooms, but this legislation was not effective.[3]

Statistics for fatal occupational accidents in England appear to be extremely scanty until late in

[16] T. R. Forbes, "Two New John Hunter Manuscripts," *Guildhall Studies London History* **1** (1973): pp. 24–27.

[17] A dresser was a senior medical student chosen to assist a surgeon in the hospital. He was allowed to perform minor surgical procedures, dress wounds, let blood, etc. W. N. B. Watson, "Thomas Robertson, Naval Surgeon, 1793–1828," *Bull. History Med.* **46** (1972): pp. 131–149. F. F. Cartwright, "Robert Bentley Todd's Contributions to Medicine," *Proc. Roy. Soc. Med.* **67** (1974): pp. 893–897.

[18] MS. 4026.

[1] George Rosen, *The History of Miners' Diseases* (New York, 1943), chap. 2.

[2] R.S.F. Schilling, *Occupational Health Practice* (1973, London), pp. 1–6; P.E.H. Hair, "Deaths from Violence in Britain: A Tentative Secular Survey," *Pop. Studies* **25** (1971): pp. 5–24.

[3] Schilling (n. 2), pp. 7–8.

the nineteenth century, data on such deaths being very seldom segregated as such.[4] John Graunt, for a reason that we would regard as incorrect, chose not to assemble statistics on fatalities related to occupation.[5]

We shall say nothing of the numbers of those, that have been drowned, killed by falls from scaffolds, or by carts running over them, & c. because the same depends upon the casual trade and employment of men, and upon matters, which are but circumstantial to the seasons and regions we live in, and affords little of that science and certainty we aim at.

Marshall also did not present statistics on occupational accidents as such, but Walford, commenting on early returns of deaths under the Registration Act, remarked that "The violent deaths of men with occupations above ground were very generally from the effects of falls, to which masons, plasterers, slaters, painters, and glaziers were found peculiarly liable."[6] Hair has assembled valuable data on industrial fatalities, mostly nonurban, in Britain, particularly for coal mines and railways.[7] The information on the following pages provides what appears to be the first detailed analysis of occupational deaths in London from 1788 to 1829.

I have defined such deaths rather broadly, choosing to include fatalities due not only directly but indirectly to occupation. Thus, for example, when a drunken sailor, returning from an evening ashore, fell into the Thames and drowned while attempting to climb the side of his ship, I have categorized this death as occupational, on the basis that the sailor's trade required him, drunk or not, to return to his vessel. The accident would not have occurred if he had not been a sailor. On the other hand, I almost certainly failed to detect the occupational aspect of some accidental deaths. Depositions as summarized were often sketchy, and it might not be stated, for example, that a woman who fell from a window was a housemaid at work or that a man found drowned in the Thames was a wherryman whose boat had been upset.

Inquisitions were seen for a total of 3,316 accidental[8] deaths (table 2). Of these, 944 were classified as occupational fatalities, all but 12 of the latter being those of males (table 3). *Falls* caused more deaths than any other cause, falls from ladders, scaffolds, and stages being particularly numerous.

A bricklayer was on a scaffold lime-washing the back of a house. The rope supporting the scaffold broke and he fell 20 feet to the ground.

When a scaffold in St. Paul's church gave way, a laborer fell 30 feet to the pavement.

TABLE 2

INQUISITIONS BY MAJOR CATEGORIES AND SEX

	Male	Female	Not Stated	Total
Accident	2529	773	14	3316
Illness	1527	372	1	1900
Suicide while lunatic	643	282		925
Suicide	15	1		16
Murder	46	32	4	82
Other homicides	41	15		56
Stillborn	15	15	10	40
Not stated	12	3	1	16
Total	4828	1493	30	6351

A laborer carrying a hod of bricks fell from a ladder.

Two laborers fell from a scaffold when it was struck by a falling timber.

A painter fell from a stage outside the third floor of a warehouse.

A laborer fell from a stage while coppering the bottom of a ship in dry dock.

A laborer was on a ladder, placing a timber to shore up a house. A passing wagon struck the timber, which toppled against the ladder, causing it to fall.

A carpenter fell from a scaffold at the top of Cold Bath Prison in St. James, Clerkenwell.

Seven laborers at work on a scaffold were helping to construct a sugar warehouse. When rain began, the men took shelter under an arch at one end of the scaffold. Part of the latter broke and three laborers fell.

A laborer fell through a trap door in the workshop of Sadlers Wells Theatre and to the stage 25 feet below.

A man standing on a scaffold in a "manufactory" where he painted floor cloth (oilcloth) fell ten feet to the ground.

A lamplighter at work fell from his ladder when the stone coping supporting it gave way.

Falls in breweries were not uncommon. Men toppled from the tops of vats and from ladders inside vats. An excise officer fell from the bridge of an upper cooler to the top of a copper vat. Other fatal accidents occurred when workers fell from lofts or through trap doors or loop holes.

A man employed to drag sacks of paper shavings with a hook to a loop hole in the third floor of a warehouse became himself entangled with the hook and fell to the floor below.

An ironmonger fell through the trap door of his shop into the cellar.

A tier boy, assistant to the printer in an oil cloth factory, fell through the "well hole which is left open for the purpose of hanging the oil cloth to dry."

A servant fell from a loft window through which he was pitching hay.

A laborer on the seventh floor of a warehouse tried to slide down a rope through a loophole to the floor below; the rope was not properly secured.

A worker was leaning against a bar in the outside door of a loft when the bar broke.

[4] Hair (n. 2); Walford, "On the Number of Deaths from Accident, Negligence, Violence, and Misadventure in the United Kingdom and Some Other Countries."

[5] Graunt, *Natural and Political Observations*, p. 13.

[6] Marshall, *Mortality of the Metropolis*; (n. 4), Walford, p. 454.

[7] Hair (n. 2), p. 21.

[8] Deaths have been categorized as due to accident, illness, etc. on the basis of the verdicts of the juries, even in the relatively small number of cases where the designation of the cause of death seems to us erroneous.

TABLE 3

ACCIDENTAL DEATHS BY CAUSE AND SEX

	Occupational		Non-Ocupational			
	Male	Female	Male	Female	Unknown	Total
Drownings						
From ship, barge	154		143	1		298
From small boat	55		101	3	1	160
Bathing			17	1		18
Miscellaneous	16		78	12		106
Manner unknown	13		326	55	1	395
	238		665	72	2	977
Falls						
On or from ship, barge	63		32	42		137
From house window, roof	49	3	55		1	108
Inside house	3		41	24		68
From or in warehouse, loft, shop, public building	41		29	3		73
From ladder, scaffold	136		6	1		143
From stationary vehicle	12		2	2		16
In street			18	11		29
From London Bridge (under construction)	17					17
Miscellaneous	11		16	5		32
	332	3	199	88	1	623
Burns						
Clothes ignited at home			166	357		523
Occupational	21	1				22
Miscellaneous			48	54	6	108
	21	1	214	411	6	653
Vehicles, Horses						
Moving vehicles	89		273	105		467
Horses	19		85	8		112
	108		358	113		579
Other						
Falling object	43		29	11		83
Crane, windlass, capstan	36		5			41
Collapse of building	36		12	10	2	60
Crushed (except by vehicle or building)	29			1		30
Machinery (except hoisting)	28	1	1			30
Asphyxiation	26		27	15		68
Buried	12			1		13
Firearm, gunpowder, fireworks	12	7	15			34
Poisoning			13	15	1	29
Crushed in crowd			27	6	2	35
Overlaid, dropped (infants)			4	6		10
Animal (except horse)			5	3		8
Explosion	2					2
Other	9		23	9		41
	233	8	161	77	5	484
Total	932	12	1597	761	14	3316

A watchman fell from the top of a cistern in the yard of the Marshalsea Prison.

Other men fell while cleaning the first-story windows of the Temple Coffee House, while painting a window in Newgate Prison, and while repairing the windows of dwelling houses.

Not surprisingly, falls on ships were fairly common. Work on the rigging was hazardous even when a vessel was at anchor in the Thames or was tied to a wharf. Ice made footing treacherous, a rotten spar gave way, a yard was brushed by the rigging of a passing vessel, or a hand simply slipped. In one case a sailor was seized with a fit while at the masthead of a ship and dropped before help could reach him. A number of men fell through open hatchways into holds while at work.

The construction of bridges across the Thames evidently was a dangerous occupation. The Southwark Bridge, 700 feet long, was erected by a private company in 1813–1819.[9] The number of men employed seems not to have been recorded, but

[9] Charles Welch, *History of the Tower Bridge* (London, 1894), pp. 143–144.

inquests on eight of them were held in 1815–1818. Deaths were due to falls when a foot slipped, a plank broke, a timber shifted, or a stone being hoisted swung out of control. There were more accidental deaths during the construction of London Bridge. The next to the latest in the series of bridges at that site was erected in the nineteenth century, construction being completed in 1831. More than 800 men worked on the job; forty of them are said to have lost their lives.[10] I found records of the inquests on ten of these deaths, dated from 1825 to 1828. Again, the fatalities were caused mostly by falls from various parts of the structure. In addition, a plank fell onto a workman, and another laborer, clearing away rubbish from the old London Bridge, located next to the site of its successor, was crushed by a collapsing arch. A bargeman was drowned when his craft upset after striking a boom placed beneath the bridge during construction. The other men killed were laborers, a carpenter, a shipwright, and three pile drivers.

Drowning, the second most frequent cause of occupational death (table 3), nearly always occurred in the Thames. The great waterway carried dozens of vessels, from small craft to merchant ships, which in the course of a day transported large numbers of people and hundreds of tons of goods, building materials, and so on. Colquhoun estimated that in 1800 commerce on the Thames gave employment, directly or indirectly, to 120,000 people and involved 22,500 vessels of all sizes. All of London's coal arrived by sea and was sold at Billingsgate. Almost all of it was removed from ships and barges by hand. Coal handling machines for unloading ships were invented in the eighteenth century, and one was tried on the Thames in 1805, but the coal-whippers felt their employment was threatened and blocked the use of such devices. They did not really come into operation until the second half of the century.[11]

Falls into the water from a ship, barge, or other large vessel caused the deaths of 154 workers, many of whom were casual labor.[12] Such accidents were usually of two kinds. Either a worker slipped while climbing between one vessel and another or between a vessel and a small boat, or he fell from a plank laid between two vessels, or a vessel and a wharf. Falls from planks most often happened as a worker was carrying a load on his back to or from the shore.

While unloading sacks of flour from a barge, a laborer fell into the Thames.

A bargeman was standing at the stern of his barge when the tiller moved suddenly, knocking him into the water.

A laborer carrying a sack of oats fell from a plank between a ship and a barge.

A porter carrying corn fell from a plank between a barge and a wharf.

A bricklayer unloading bricks from a barge was struck by a falling mast and knocked into the river.

Two laborers were carrying barrels of saltpeter on a plank between river stairs and a barge when one of them slipped into the swift current.

Other workers who toppled from planks and drowned had been carrying coal, potatoes, or brimstone.

Watermen rowed or sailed great numbers of small boats that transported passengers or goods or both.

Two men were towing timber up river with a skiff when it was upset by the swift current. One man was drowned.

A boatman sculling his small craft on the Thames thrust his oar too far into the water so that he was overpowered and forced into the river.

A wherryman was pushed out of his boat when it got athwart the bowsprit rigging of a ship.

A sudden squall unshipped the mast of a lighter. The mast fell, striking a sailor in a wherry being towed behind the lighter and knocking him into the Thames.

The wind having failed, several men were in a boat towing a ship up the river. The boat became jammed between this ship and another that was aground, and one man fell into the water.

A waterman trying to push his boat free from a starling of London Bridge fell into the Thames when his oar broke.

The starlings were indirectly responsible for a number of accidents. The "old" London Bridge had been built by Peter de Colechurch, a priest, beginning in 1176. At that time a starling was made by driving pilings into the bed of the river in the outline of a boat pointed up and down stream. After the timbers were bolted together, the enclosure was filled with large stones, and the massive structure provided a base for a pier of the bridge. From an engineering standpoint the starlings were very effective—the bridge lasted for 653 years—but because the arches of London Bridge were short, there had to be nineteen of them, resting on twenty piers and starlings, to support the 926-foot-long structure. The starlings acted like a series of short dams, except at high tide, reducing the free passage for the Thames by more than two-thirds. Since when the tide is running the current is rather swift even in the unobstructed river, the flow between the starlings at times was like a rapids, and to "shoot the starlings" was perilous indeed. Samuel Johnson advised, "London Bridge was made for wise men to go over and fools to go under."[13]

A few bodies found in the river were identified as those of sailors who had drowned. I classified these as occupational deaths. A small number of drownings did not take place in the Thames. A bizarre accident, for example, occurred in a brewery when an excise

[10] (N. 9), p. 130. This bridge, in turn, was replaced in 1969.

[11] P. Colquhoun, *A Treatise on the Commerce and Police of the River Thames* (London, 1800), pp. xxx, 15; Raymond Smith, *Sea-coal for London* (London, 1961), pp. xii, 288–289; Francis Sheppard, *London 1808–1870: The Infernal Wen* (London, 1971), pp. 192–193.

[12] Sheppard (n. 11), pp. 364–365.

[13] *London Bridge* (London, 1971), unpaged. Peter Jackson, *London Bridge* (London, 1971), pp. 9, 71.

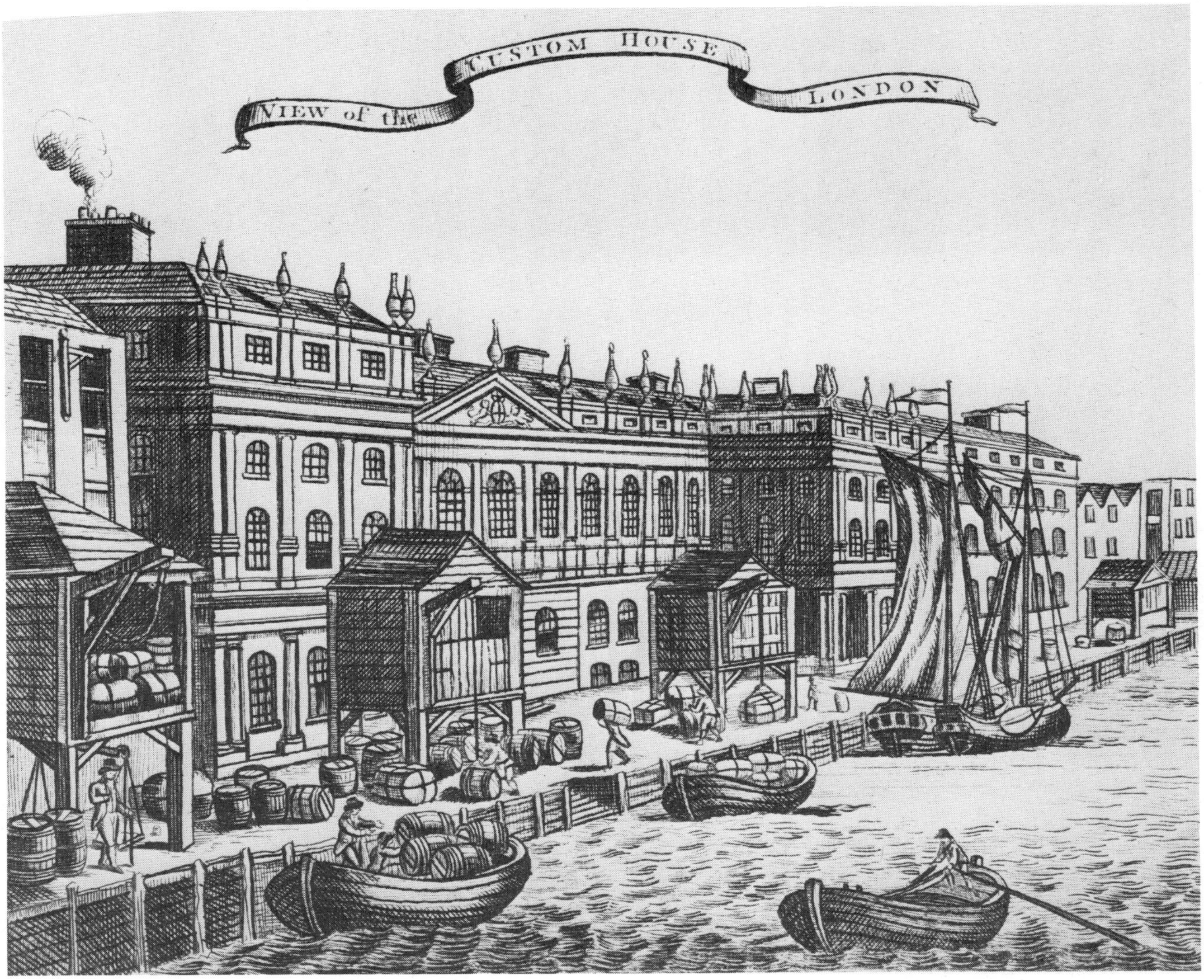

FIG. 2. A busy London wharf with its workers, cranes, wherries, ships, and cargoes. Edward Langley, 1810–1820. Courtesy of Guildhall Library, City of London.

officer fell into an underground reservoir containing 100 barrels of fermenting beer.

Burns were responsible for more than twenty occupational deaths. Nearly all occurred when workmen fell into vats of hot fluids. It is difficult to be sure why adequate precautions were not always taken against such obvious and deadly hazards.

A worker employed to skim the surface of a copper of boiling oil in a leather dresser's shop fell in.

A carpenter was at work on boards placed over a vat in which cut logwood was extracted for dyeing hats. The boards broke.

A laborer at Greenland Dock was skimming the contents of a copper vat in which whale blubber was being boiled when he slipped.

In His Majesty's Dockyard in Deptford a laborer fell into a large vessel of boiling water in which timbers were soaked so that they could be bent. Other laborers fell into vats of hot liquid in grease manufactories, a hat manufactory, and several distilleries. One or two victims were reported to have been drinking. Another had a fit as he was stirring a hot mixture of malt and sugar in a brewery.

A servant girl fumigated a bed with two pans containing burning charcoal and brimstone "to destroy bugs." Evidently she spilled some coals, for later the house burst into flames and the girl perished.

At least five men were fatally burned when alcohol in one form or another escaped and became ignited.

A still was being charged with spirits; the latter overflowed and ran into the stoke hole where a fire burned.

"Spirits of wine" spilled in a cabinet-making shop and reached the fire that heated the glue pot; two men died.

The head cellarman of a distillery was supervising the mixing of 670 gallons of rum when a cock near the bottom of the vat came loose. The clerk tried to stop the flow and another worker came to help. Unfortunately he was carrying a lighted candle.

Contemporary illustrations make it clear that principal streets could be crowded with wagons, coaches, carts, horses, and pedestrians. Accidents caused by *vehicles and horses* were common; often such incidents involved men at work. Many drivers who came to grief were asleep, had been drinking, or took chances. Horses were not always under control. Few accidents to pedestrians were occupational, although at least one crossing sweeper was run over by a cart.

Many drivers lost their lives when they fell from their vehicles.

A coachman fell from his lofty box after the horses bolted and a wheel came off. He was then run over by his own coach.

While a two-horse cart loaded with bricks was moving, the driver tried to climb onto the shaft. He fell, was crushed by his cart.

The clothes of a carter became caught in a hook in the harness. He was dragged to the ground and run over.

A horse bolted. The driver, walking beside his vehicle, was crushed between it and a post.

A horse pulling a cart load of old kettles ran away when a kettle fell onto his back. The driver, apparently leading the horse, was knocked down by the shaft and run over by a wheel.

A wagoner, asleep and seated on the shaft of his moving wagon, fell off and was run over.

A drayman seated with his legs over the side of his vehicle had one of them crushed between the dray and the post of a turnpike.

A drunken driver fell off his cart and was run over.

A wagoner seated on the shaft fell to the street and was crushed after he had whipped his horses.

A dustman walking beside his cart fell and was run over.

The driver of a fire engine who was riding on the shaft fell to the ground and was run over by the hind wheel.

FIG. 3. Accidents are always a threat in a busy city thoroughfare, as in this view by T. S. Boys of Fleet Street in 1842. Note the artist's name on the wagon. Courtesy of Guildhall Library, City of London.

FIG. 4. Thomas Rowlandson's satirical street scene portrays a variety of hazards for the Londoner of 1807. Even the sign over the gold beater's door seems none too secure. Courtesy of Guildhall Library, City of London.

The driver of a carriage transporting a fire engine belonging to the Phoenix Fire Office in Morgan Street was intoxicated, whipped the horses, fell off, and was killed. The deposition does not say whether the vehicle was going to a fire.

A truck carrying stones on a kind of railway in a stone yard ran over a worker.

Clearly, since a driver by necessity often walked or rode just in front of the wheels, he was in peril when he fell to the street unless the horses could be stopped instantly. Thus even a slowly moving vehicle was a potential hazard. No doubt it was easy for a weary carter to fall asleep.

Horses and mules themselves could be dangerous.

A postboy died after the mare he was riding slipped, fell, and rolled on him.

A groom running with a mare to show it for sale was accidentally trampled.

A coachman died from the kick of a horse.

An hostler was kicked by a gelding in a stable.

Falling objects were responsible for a good many fatal accidents.

A kilderkin (half barrel) of porter being lowered by tackle into the hold of brig became unhooked, striking a man in the hold and driving a crowbar in his hand through his body.

A tackle fastened for hoisting to the top of a ship's mast gave way, fell on the head of a man on deck, and knocked him into the hold.

A packet of hops being hoisted from a cart into a warehouse fell onto the cart, shaking it. The driver was thrown to the street and was fatally injured.

A sack of flour being hoisted into a flour mill fell from its chain and struck a laborer.

A workman on a scaffold dropped a piece of iron pipe. It struck another workman on the ground.

A stone coping fell from the top of a house onto a man hired to repair it.

While workmen were raising a chandelier into position in a church, a lead counterweight broke loose and fell on one of them.

A laborer lowering a portable forge from a warehouse had wound the rope several times around an iron pipe to help to check the descent. The pipe broke and the rope forced the pipe to roll over him.

Two men were demolishing the second story of a building. Some of the debris fell onto a joist. It hit another joist, which struck one man on the head.

Falling through the trap door of a druggist's warehouse, a worker reached for a cask of ginger to save himself. It fell on him.

A laborer was repairing a tank holding 752 tons of water at the South London Gas Manufactory. The tank suddenly burst and the water struck him down, causing a head injury.

Cranes, windlasses, and capstans accounted for 36 deaths. A windlass turns on a horizontal axle; a capstan, on a vertical one. Both devices were sometimes used to pull the rope of a crane. Nearly always, the capstan was turned by men pushing on horizontal bars set into the upper end of the drum that wound the rope. The drum of a properly constructed windlass or capstan could be held in check by a ratchet and pawl. Accidents could happen when a heavy weight was being raised or lowered if the capstan lacked a ratchet and pawl or the pawl was not engaged. Or a capstan bar could break.

Five men had pushed on the bars of a capstan "belonging to a Crane fixed to an upper Warehouse . . . to hoist up by the said Crane a Cask of Oil of great weight . . . to the door-way of the said Warehouse . . . it so happened that the said Cask slipt from the said door-way and by the weight thereof the said Bars were forced around with great velocity and the . . . men so being at the said Bars were struck and knocked down with the said Bars to the floor. . . ." The cask weighed about one and a half tons. One of the men was fatally injured.

In another type of hoisting device, the walking wheel crane, the rope was wound on a windlass. Also fixed on the horizontal shaft was a huge double wheel with steps inside its periphery on which men could walk. As they climbed or descended the steps, the wheel and windlass turned accordingly. The arrangement somewhat resembled a treadmill, but the workers were within the wheel. A seventeenth-century crane at Harwich, for example, had two wheels about sixteen feet in diameter and three and a half feet wide. The two wheels, which turned on the same shaft with the windlass drum between them, each accommodated twelve men.[14] While this type of crane must have been quite powerful, it was dangerous. One writer commented in 1810:[15]

> It is a well-known though melancholy fact, that numbers of unfortunate persons have lost their lives in the walking-wheel cranes, by their canting back, when overpowered by the weight craning up; for the men having no means whereby to save themselves, their destruction is inevitable.

A Mr. Joseph Dixon of London invented a "preservative wheel" consisting of a trapeze-like bar suspended by two loops of rope from the shaft inside the wheel and hanging free. The idea was that, if the wheel began to turn out of control, the men "may suspend themselves, with the greatest safety, till all danger is past." It is difficult to understand how up to twelve men could manage to hang from such a bar. In addition, someone pointed out, as human weight was removed from the wheel it would spin faster and faster, exposing workers still inside, nearby, or under the load to great danger. Wheels in the Thames-side cranes were said to be about 15 feet in diameter.[15]

A man in a walking wheel crane was lowering a barrel of porter from a quay into the hold of a ship when the crane suddenly stopped. The man was found with his head caught between a spoke of the crane and an upright post.

Four men were in a wheel hoisting heavy bales of linen from a lighter. When the signal was given to lower the bales onto the wharf, two men stepped out of the wheel. As the latter began to spin, one of the remaining pair managed to save himself. The other "being an Old Man the Wheel went round to fast for him so that he fell down in consequence of which the Wheel went round so swift the deced [deceased] was thrown from one part of the Wheel to the other until the Goods were again landed in the Lighter."

A cask of sugar was being lowered into a vessel on the Thames when the wheel began to spin. Because of the inexperience of one of the two men inside they lost control. One worker managed to cling to the spokes until the wheel stopped; the other was thrown out and killed. Both of these men, it developed, were soldiers in the Foot Guards.[16] Apparently they had been put to work as casual labor without adequate instruction.

Another kind of crane accident occurred when two men were unloading sacks of seed from a barge with a rope worked by a steam engine.[17] While one laborer was steadying a sack to be hoisted, the engine raised it very quickly. He made the mistake of not at once letting go

> and keeping his hold of the Sack was drawn up with it, that when the Sack had got to the Door of the Loft it was to be taken in at (being four story high) the deced let go his hold and fell down upon the deck of the Barge.

A bargeman was using a windlass to lower the mast on his barge before it went under London Bridge. He was too late. The mast struck the bridge, forcing the windlass to turn violently backward. The handle of the windlass killed the bargeman.

The *collapse of buildings* or of parts of buildings caused fatalities. Inquests were held on 21, 23, and 26 September, 1808, on the bodies of seven men, apparently firemen, who died during the blaze in Covent Garden Theatre on 20–21 September or in the hospital as a result of their injuries. The men were operating the pumps on a fire engine that had been moved "into the Passage leading from the Piazza to the Theatre" when the roof collapsed. Other firemen died during conflagrations when parts of private houses or of a coffee house fell on them. Floors or walls collapsed in buildings that were being torn down and caused the deaths of laborers. Less understandably, houses under construction also fell, killing carpenters and bricklayers. Other workers lost their lives when large piles of chalk or sand piled against walls caused their sudden collapse.

---

[14] D. W. Clark, "A Crane of Pepysian Times," *Country Life*, 28 Dec., 1929 [no pagination]; D. W. Clark, "The Harwich Crane," *Essex Review* **62** (1933): pp. 1–15; John Wilkes, *Encyclopaedia Londinensis* (London, 1810) **5**: pp. 321–322.

[15] Wilkes (n. 14), p. 322; A. Rees, *The Cyclopaedia* (London, 1819) **3**, no pagination; **10**, no pagination; Joseph Glynn, *Rudimentary Treatise on the Construction of Cranes* (London, 1854), pp. 26–28.

[16] I encountered several other instances of private employment of soldiers on the wharves.

[17] This was in 1802, when industrial use of such engines must still have been fairly new.

Fatal *crushing injuries* were not uncommon.

A laborer had loaded a cart with earth from an excavation. As he stooped behind the cart, a large mass of earth rolled on him.

Employees of a wholesale ironmonger were unloading a heavy bar of iron, standing it on one end. It toppled, crushing one man.

A dock worker was moving stacks of clover seed. Pigs of copper stacked against the sacks fell over, one of them on him.

The back of a laborer was broken when the full weight of a timber he was unloading suddenly came on him.

Porters and others on occasion undertook huge loads and could be overwhelmed.

A workman was carrying a stone on his back. When it slipped, he was crushed.

A laborer with a basket of fish on his head fell backward on London Bridge. The basket struck his lower abdomen.

While carrying a large piece of iron at a dockyard, a worker jumped five feet from a plank to the ground. The iron fell on him.

A laborer with a crate of oranges on his back fell in the street just outside a warehouse and was fatally injured by his load.

A chest of oranges weighing 225–250 pounds was placed on a "knot"[18] on a porter's head. Going down the warehouse steps he slipped. The crate fractured a cervical vertebra.

In an almost identical accident, the chest of lemons carried by one man weighed over 300 pounds.

Machinery except for hoisting caused 28 occupational deaths.

The wheel of an engine belonging to the Portable Gas Co. caught a worker and forced him against the frame.

A man became tangled in the machinery of a flatting mill.

The clothes of a laborer became caught between the stones of a drug mill in the cellar of a manufacturing chemist.

A boy whose task it was to feed woolen ropes into a breaker machine that manufactured flocks caught his hand between the rollers.

The operator of a mechanical swing at a fair fell and was struck by the swing.

Horses provided the power for a foundry machine, a fabric-glazing machine, a gypsum grinder, and a flatting mill for rolling gold and silver into sheets; fatal accidents occurred with all this machinery. Curiously enough, the victim of the flatting mill was not employed there but had been hired to pave the stable behind the mill. To get to his work he had to pass close to the mill while it was being turned; he was crushed by a harness yoke on a horse. In addition to fatal accidents due to machinery powered by horses, at least fourteen men were killed in accidents with steam machinery. Of the latter episodes, one occurred in 1803, six in 1815–1819, and eight in 1821–1827, reflecting the increasing use of steam engines. Four of the deaths happened when boilers burst, the victims usually being engine operators. In one accident with an engine of a new design, it was reported that four men were killed and three were hurt. (I found the inquisition for only one of the four deaths.) Parts of the boiler weighing three hundred pounds were thrown 90 to 100 yards. In the remaining cases, workers fell into or were caught in moving parts of a stationary steam engine or of machines for shredding fabrics, chopping sausage meat, grinding chemicals, brushing cloth, pumping water, and hoisting ballast. A stoker fell into the engine of a steam packet.

Asphyxia from carbon monoxide and other gases caused numerous occupational deaths. The most common occurrence was for sailors in a ship at anchor to make a charcoal fire in a stove in the forecastle to keep warm. All the accidents happened at night when the men went to sleep after shutting the hatch. The next morning they would be missed and the forecastle would be found to be filled with fumes. Sometimes the sailors had even covered the opening through which the smoke was supposed to escape. Heavy drinking was a contributing factor in some instances.

There were other fatal accidents due to asphyxia.

Fumigation of a ship with the gases from burning charcoal to kill the rats was begun and the crew left the vessel.[19] One of them unwisely returned.

Two laborers were employed to fumigate a wine cellar under a house with burning charcoal. Both men became unconscious. Only one of them recovered enough to crawl to safety.

A gang of men was hired to remove the lees from a large soap reservoir in a factory. In the vat "there was a great quantity of noxious and unwholesome Air." One man was overcome and collapsed. A fellow worker who tried to rescue him died.

In a similar accident, two men cleaning the residue from a vat of "iron liquor"[20] were asphyxiated.

Six night-soil men came to a house at midnight to empty the pit of a privy by lowering buckets from above. At 3:40 A.M. one worker, in spite of warnings, descended into the pit and lost consciousness. A second man climbed down a ladder to help him and also collapsed. Both men were removed but could not be revived.

The straw in a well where ice was stored caught fire, possibly from a lantern let down for an inspection. Several men were lowered, apparently successively, to put out the fire. One of them was overcome by fumes. He and a would-be rescuer both perished.

Accidents to *chimney sweeps* are among the saddest that are recorded. Much of the work was done by young boys, chosen for their small size, appren-

[18] A pad for cushioning and supporting a load.

[19] Obviously the potentially lethal effect of charcoal fumes was recognized.

[20] Ferrous acetate solution, used as a mordant by calico printers.

ticed into a dangerous and terrifying trade, forced to work long hours, and, it is said, deliberately malnourished to retard their growth. If they survived suffocation in a flue, they could live to develop pulmonary tuberculosis or cancer of the scrotum.[21] Most heat for homes came from coal burned in fireplaces. The flues of the latter were led into chimneys. Sometimes a confusing arrangement of passages resulted, and a chimney sweep could become lost.

Two sweeps, one aged thirteen and one nine or ten, were sent up an oven flue leading to a chimney in a bakery to clear away rubbish. The debris gave way, falling on the younger boy, who was dead when he was removed. The older boy was stuck in the chimney for nearly two hours. Two cups of water were passed up to him, but he also was dead when he was extricated.

A boy aged between nine and ten was sent up to sweep the chimney of a bedroom. He did not return because, it transpired, he had lost his way and come down the wrong flue. He refused to descend to his master, fearing a beating. The master thereupon went to the roof and poured a pail of water down the chimney on the child to drive him out. At the same time, the master afterward deposed, his "foot slipped" and some pieces of brick "fell" down the chimney, striking the boy on the head. He then came down and was sent to sweep the chimney of an alehouse. Later "the boy was coming into the Tap room, and he appeared to be wet and cold and he attempted to go near the fire but his Master would not let him." But he "appeared to be well and did not complain" and was put to sweeping yet another chimney. The next day he spoke of cuts on his head and the master sweep "washed the Lads head with a little of his own Chamber lye" (urine).

About ten days later the boy, who "appeared unwell," went only a short distance up a chimney. When he failed to climb higher, the master sweep sent another boy up. He found the first sweep caught in the chimney and could not free him. At the master's direction a rope was then tied to the trapped boy's legs and his master pulled him down. He was taken to a surgeon but died a little later.

A chimney sweep was sent down a brewhouse chimney from the roof after the fire in the fireplace had been swept out. Soon after, the boy "called out and sayed Master I can't come up—I must die here." A rope was lowered to him but he could only be raised a short distance. The master then got a bricklayer to break away the brick work of the chimney. The boy was dead. The bricklayer deposed that he thought "*it was a ten inch flew, and that it was big enough for the boy*, but that the Boy was suffocated."[22]

Cave-ins occurred when excavations were being dug or gravel was being removed from pits, and sometimes *burial* of a laborer resulted. Usually the accident happened because the side of the hole was undermined. Death was due to suffocation or crushing or both.

Firearms, gunpowder, and fireworks caused the deaths of nineteen workers.

An apprentice was cleaning a musket in the gun room of a ship. The weapon was accidentally discharged, fatally injuring a second apprentice. The first boy said he did not know the gun was loaded.

A watchman accidentally shot himself with one of his pistols.

An apprentice said he was in the habit of firing a pistol at night to frighten people away from a house being built for his master. While holding the gun, he fell and shot himself.

The owner of a manufactory protected it at night from robbers with a spring gun loaded with gunpowder and paper. A sixteen-year-old apprentice whose task it was to set up and remove the gun shot himself.

A gunsmith was cleaning a bundle of used gun barrels by heating them in a furnace. One barrel was loaded. The powder exploded and the bullet struck the gunsmith.

A shop for making fireworks in the ground floor of a house caught fire at night. Three male and six female employees asleep in the upper floors were trapped and died.

Two fireworks makers died in a shop when the rocket that one of them was filling with "Gunpowder and other Combustibles" caught fire. An explosion followed. One of the victims was a journeyman lamplighter.

Two other employees died in an almost identical accident. It was reported that 20 to 30 pounds of gunpowder were stored in the shop.

On the high seas a cannon on the sloop of war *Speedy* was accidentally discharged. The ball struck a brig and injured a sailor. When his ship reached London, he was taken to St. Thomas's Hospital, where he died two weeks after his injury.

It was of course rare for an inquest on a death originating at sea to come to a London coroner.

Miscellaneous occupational accidents, some of them bizarre, accounted for a few other deaths.

In a steam boiler factory, a helper held a punch in position for his fellow to strike with a sledge hammer. As the latter swung his sledge, he asked the helper to step aside. The helper did so, but into rather than out of the path of the sledge.

Two men were employed to pump foul water out of a gasometer (gasholder) at the Coburg Theatre in Lambeth.[23] When someone brought a lighted candle too close, there was an explosion and the two men were crushed between the top of the gasometer and the ceiling of the theater.

[21] S. X. Radbill, "A History of Child Abuse and Infanticide," in: R. E. Helfer and C. H. Kempe, eds., *The Battered Child* (Chicago, 1968), p. 12. Chimney sweep's cancer was described by Percivall Pott, the distinguished London surgeon, in 1775. It was one of the first reports of an occupational cancer.

[22] Italics added.

[23] Presumably the gasometer, a storage tank for gas, was inside the theater to provide a supply for the numerous lights.

A carpenter fell from a bench and was fatally stabbed by the chisel he was holding.

A woman servant was gored by a cow.

A sailor on the main topsail yard of a ship at sea was struck by lightning. He fell, badly burned, into the main topsail, was brought ashore, and died there of his injuries.

A jeweler swallowed oxalic acid in his shop, mistaking the poison for digestive salts.

A bell ringer was killed in the belfry of his church when he was crushed in the wooden mechanism for ringing the bell.

A new rope, fastened to an iron block on a post, was being stretched by a team of horses to make the rope more pliant. The iron block flew off the post and struck the ironmonger's apprentice.

Alcoholic intoxication was a not uncommon factor in accidental deaths, most commonly in falls from ships, barges, houses, and so on. Drunkenness may have occurred more often than was apparent; deponents at inquests often showed an understandable reluctance to state that a fellow employee was "in liquor." Hard drinking was a common feature of the social scene.[24]

What we would call employer liability was seldom the subject of comment at an inquest. While it was the duty of the coroner to determine the circumstances of death, he seems usually not to have been much concerned with the possible contributory negligence of an employer. Such disinterest would have been consonant with a general public attitude that tolerated twelve- to fifteen-hour working days for unskilled and semi-skilled men, women, and children, sometimes under appalling conditions and for wages barely enough to sustain life. Sick, injured, or dead employees could easily be replaced from an ample pool of the unemployed.[25] Casual laborers, not adequately instructed, were sometimes expected to use complicated machinery deficient in safety devices.[26]

The depositions made at the inquests occasionally include a little information as to what happened to fatally injured or sick individuals in the interval before death. Frequently assistance was sent for from a surgeon, physician, or apothecary. It was common practice to attempt to bleed an unconscious person, partly, it appears, because bleeding was considered beneficial and partly because failure of blood to flow was recognized as an indication that the victim had died. There were many attempts to draw blood from drowned persons.

We cannot of course determine how many individuals who fell into the Thames were rescued. Sometimes resuscitation was attempted.

A woman was pulled from the river with a boat hook at Billingsgate Quay. She "groaned very much but could not speak." The woman was carried on the deponent's back to the Antigallican[27] Public House. She was refused a bed but allowed to sit before the fire and "in a little time . . . recovered and asked for her shoes." She departed and died the next morning.

A drowned boy was taken to the same place, "a House appointed by the Humane Society for the reception of drowned persons."

In another drowning case reference was made to "the Fortune of War Publick House which is a receiving house appointed by the Humane Society."

Unfortunately, there is no further information in the depositions about the Humane Society and no hint as to the technique of resuscitation.[28] I found no mention of a postmortem examination of a drowned person.[29]

Injured or ill persons were often taken to the hospital, being transported by coach, on a shutter or door, or even on a man's back.[30] Depositions by surgeons, dressers, apothecaries, and others seldom describe medical treatment, usually referring simply to "the measures usual in such a case." It is of interest that trepanning was sometimes performed for head injuries.

A laborer who fell from a scaffold struck his head. At St. Bartholomew's Hospital trepanning disclosed a quantity of coagulated blood.

A similar accident resulted in multiple skull fractures. The surgeon trephined[31] his patient "in order to try whether any effusion had taken place and which was the only means of affording assistance."

The nature of the original injury, the time interval between injury and death, and brief comments on the patient's course in the hospital make it clear that infection repeatedly intervened to turn a seemingly good recovery into a fatal decline. This was a common occurrence, for example, after a compound fracture.

A man employed with others to break up a ship had his leg crushed when a steel porthole fell on it. In a few days "a serious inflammation succeeded." The leg was amputated but "mortification" developed and he died twenty-one days after his injury.

A piece of iron being raised with a crane in a foundry slipped and fell on a laborer's foot. He did well at first in hospital, then erysipelas and mortification appeared. He died eleven days after he was hurt.

A workman's ankle was crushed by a falling timber. He was cared for in hospital "but an inflammation came on which diffused all over him and killed him" twelve days after he was hurt.

During the construction of a bridge across the Serpentine in Hyde Park, a sheerlegs fell on a workman's foot. In the hospital he "did very well for a

[24] Sheppard (n. 11), pp. 367–368; Hair, "Accidental Death and Suicide in Shropshire 1780–1809."

[25] Sheppard (n. 11), pp. 364–365. It was not until 1833, for example, that children under nine years of age were prohibited from working in factories (n. 4, Walford).

[26] Schilling (n. 2), pp. 5–6.

[27] That is, opposed to what is French.

[28] The Royal Humane Society had established "places appointed for receiving persons apparently drowned or dead, and at which drags and other apparatus are kept." (Charles Dickens, *Dicken's Dictionary of London* (London, 1880), p. 137.)

[29] Postmortem examinations will be discussed later.

[30] Deaths in hospital will be considered in a subsequent chapter.

[31] The trephine was an improved form of the trepan.

considerable time." Then a "violent purging" ensued. He died twenty-nine days after the accident.

A large stone being unloaded from a cart crushed a laborer's fingers. He was recovering in the hospital when "symptoms of Tetanus or locked jaw came on" and he died eight days after being injured.

After the registration of deaths began, statistics on violent death were published annually by the Registrar General from 1838 to 1842. Then there was an interruption, but annual publication of the numbers of violent deaths was resumed in 1848 and continued thereafter. The report for 1840 had included the distribution of deaths by accident and violence according to the occupation of the deceased but did not indicate which deaths were occupational, a quite different matter.[32] Some recognition of statistics on occupational deaths in England had emerged by 1856, when deaths in mines were separately categorized by the Registrar General.[33] Hair[34] has recently called attention to occupational accidents, particularly those occurring in mines and quarries and those caused by machinery, as significant contributors to deaths by violence in Britain in the eighteenth and nineteenth centuries.[34]

IV. ACCIDENTAL DEATHS NOT RELATED TO OCCUPATION

The most frequent cause of non-occupational accidental death was *drowning* (table 3). Nearly all such fatalities were in the Thames. Individuals were seen to fall from barges, ships, and boats of all sizes into the river.

Several passengers in a skiff were drowned when it was struck and upset by a barge.

A boy fell from a small boat passing under London Bridge, because of the "great fall and violence of the water." The tide was running swiftly.

A wherry was struck and sunk by the paddles of the Thames-Gravesend Steamboat. A passenger in the wherry drowned.

However, many other drownings in the Thames—nearly half the total number—were not observed, the body only being found some time later, and in these cases it could not be determined just how death occurred. Because there was sometimes the possibility that drowning might have been due to suicide or to homicide, the body and the pockets of the victim were often examined.

A corpse found on a mud flat when the tide was out showed no marks of violence. In a pocket were 3d. and a knife.

In the pockets of a body recovered from the water were a watch and a few coins.

A drowned man had a small tin box and a few papers on his person. When last seen alive by a friend "the deced appeared to be very low and dejected."

Exceptionally, there was mention in a deposition of an official effort to identify a body.

The body of a drowned woman was found in the Thames near the Custom House; "every pains has been taken by distributing hand bills and otherwise to discover who she was but without effect."

Eighteen unwary bathers were known to have lost their lives in the Thames when they went beyond their depth or were carried away by the tide. Not surprisingly, all but two of these accidents occurred during June, July, or August.

Babies and small children drowned when they fell into pits filled with water, cisterns, wells, ponds, and even pans of water.

As with the occupational drownings, there were attempts at resuscitation.

A hospital dresser tried to inflate the lungs of a drowned man and "used the means recommended by the Humane Society."

A drowned man was taken "to the Anchor Public House which is a House of reception for drowned persons."

Data cited by Walford and by Farr from the London Bills of Mortality show that drownings constituted 32.2 per cent of all violent deaths in 1647–1700, 31.4 per cent in 1701–1749, 41.9 per cent in 1750–1799, and 36.6 per cent in 1800–1829.[1] The Bills of Mortality were for metropolitan London; it is not clear why the proportions of drownings to all violent deaths reported in the Bills is relatively high. In our series of inquisitions for the City of London and Southwark in 1788–1829, the 977 drownings constitute 29.5 per cent of all accidental deaths and 23.4 per cent of deaths from accidents and violence of all kinds.[2] Of the accidental deaths reported in the *Gentleman's Magazine* for 1806, almost one-fifth were due to drowning.[3] According to the *Sixth Annual Report of the Registrar General*, of 1,016 deaths by violence exclusive of ascertained suicide in metropolitan London in 1840, 252, or 24.8 per cent, were "Accidentally Drowned" or "Found Drowned."[4] It is of interest that the annual number of City and Southwark drownings diminished between 1788 and 1829 (table 4), a period when the population of London approximately doubled.[5] In England and Wales in 1972, by contrast, drownings constituted only 1.7 per cent of all deaths from violent causes.[6]

Burns were second only to drowning as a non-occupational cause of death (table 3). Most commonly

[32] *Sixth annual report of the Registrar General*, pp. 210, 234–239.

[33] Walford (n. 4).

[34] (N. 2, 24.)

[1] Walford, p. 450. Farr, *Statistics*, p. 288. The Thames, incidentally, had long been recognized as a hazard to bathers. A royal proclamation of 1350 forbade bathing in the Thames near the Tower or in the *fosses* (ditches) on pain of death (R.R. Sharpe, *Calendar of Coroners' Rolls of the City of London, A.D. 1300–1378* (1913, London), p. xxiv).

[2] That is, accident, suicide, and homicide. See table 3.

[3] Hair, 1971: p. 13.

[4] *Sixth Annual Report*, pp. 232–233.

[5] Hogg, *London*, p. 196.

[6] *Registrar General's Review*, 1974, Part I, table 18C.

TABLE 4

ACCIDENTAL DEATH BY CAUSE, SEX, AND PERIOD

	1788–1794	1795–1802	1803–1809	1810–1816	1817–1823	1824–1829	Total
Drownings							
M	164	145	157	157	154	126	903
F	11	11	16	9	15	10	72
	175	156	173	166	169	136	975
Falls							
M	50	35	79	98	124	141	527
F	7	11	9	24	19	21	91
	57	46	88	122	143	162	618
Burns							
M	13	12	19	41	69	81	235
F	17	15	31	75	127	147	412
	30	27	50	116	196	228	647
Vehicles, Horses							
M	52	50	70	74	112	112	470
F	18	11	19	10	26	29	113
	70	61	89	84	138	141	583
Other							
M	24	42	70	58	91	109	394
F	18	5	19	12	16	15	85
	42	47	89	70	107	124	479
Total	374	337	489	558	753	791	3302[1]

[1] Does not include 14 deaths of unspecified sex.

the clothes of the victim, who was nearly always a young child or an aged person and was usually female, were ignited. Pinafores were worn by most little girls and some little boys, and these garments easily caught fire when they touched a flame. It must be remembered that fireplaces were used not only in the cold months for warmth but throughout the year for cooking and for heating water for tea. The very young and the very old were incautious and, if an accident occurred and no able-bodied adult was close by, fatal injuries were often received before help came. Repeatedly, youngsters were left alone or with other small children, sometimes in a locked room. Some victims were able to tell what happened.

While a ten-year-old girl was taking a saucepan of potatoes off a fire, her pinafore was ignited.

A little boy was lifting a slate from a mantelpiece when his pinafore caught fire.

A small girl was blowing the fire. A coal flew out on her clothes.

A girl's dress caught fire when she reached for a ball of cotton on the mantelpiece.

A five-year-old girl tried to get tea from a pot on the hearth and came too close to the flames.

"The Child said he was drying his Pin Cloth [pinafore] and that he caught fire. No one was in the house with him, his Grandmother having gone out for Porter."

The clothes of a fifty-four-year-old woman were ignited by a spark from the pipe she was smoking.

A bedridden woman was looking for her snuff box when the candle she held came too close to the curtain.

A woman had an epileptic fit and fell into the fireplace.

A woman was melting a mixture of beeswax and turpentine at the fireplace for an unction when the liquid boiled over and was ignited.

A child "worked in a Manufactory and usually came home about nine at night or a little afterward. [That night] her parents were out at the market." Her clothes caught fire.

Many persons trapped in burning buildings died inside or received fatal injuries when they jumped from a window.[7] Sometimes several people died in the same fire.

Five persons perished in an early morning fire at the Red Lion Tavern.

Four persons died in a dwelling house fire.

A mother and daughter suffocated or were burned in the attic of a house on fire.

All the occupants of a burning dwelling escaped except the housekeeper, who lived on the top floor. She delayed to save some clothes and her Leghorn bonnet.

A woman jumped from a second-floor window of a blazing house. (In an unusual statement, the coroner ruled that she died while "lawfully and justifiably seeking for her safety," i.e., she could not be considered a suicide.)

Six people sleeping on the top floor of a rooming house lost their lives in a fire.

Among all violent deaths, those for burning and scalding constituted 5 and 10 per cent in Shropshire in 1780–1784 and 1805–1809, respectively, and 22 per cent in England in the 1850's.[8] The Bills of Mortality yield proportions for London of 3.9 per cent in 1647–1700, 3.1 per cent in 1701–1749, 5.5 per cent in 1750–1799, and 11.6 per cent in 1800–1829.[9] The figure for London in 1840 was 23.8 per cent.[10] The inquisitions spell out more conspicuously the remarkable increase in the incidence of burns in the nineteenth century (table 4). Total deaths from this cause increased more than seven-fold between 1788 and 1829, a period when London's population approximately doubled.[5] Also noteworthy is the large majority of female deaths throughout the period of increase (table 4). There were 744 deaths in metropolitan London from burns and scalds in 1750–1799 and 1,150 in 1800–1829.[9] While it is clear, as

[7] Obviously, not all persons killed as a result of fires in buildings died of burns alone. However, it seemed best to include these deaths in this category.

[8] (N. 3), p. 20.

[9] (N. 1), Walford, pp. 450–451.

[10] (N. 4), pp. 210–211.

Hair points out, that fire became a serious domestic hazard in the early days of England's industrialization,[11] the reason is less apparent. Contributory factors certainly included the kind of dress worn by young children and the practice of leaving them and the aged at home with insufficient or no supervision. Accidents caused by fires, a category not identical with accidents involving burning and scalding, constituted only 3.3 per cent of all deaths from violence in England and Wales in 1972.[12]

Fatalities involving moving *vehicles and horses* were common and constituted the third largest category of accidental deaths (table 3). London's streets, many of them narrow, were often choked with traffic.[13] Stage coach accidents were fairly numerous, partly because these large vehicles were driven rapidly whenever possible, carried passengers on the roof, and sometimes had to pass through low, narrow arches when going in and out of inn yards.

While a woman was climbing a ladder to the roof of a four-horse coach, the team moved. She and the ladder fell to the ground.

A coach passenger riding on the box as it passed under an arch failed, although warned, to duck his head low enough.

A boy "catching" a ride at the back of a coach became caught in the spokes and was thrown to the ground.

A drunken sailor fell from the top of a coach.

When the horses pulling a mail coach shied, the vehicle overturned. A passenger was thrown off.

A child was run over by a coach.

A man was knocked down by the team of a coach and was crushed by a wheel.

Additional victims fell from other kinds of vehicles and were run over. Pedestrians were knocked down in the street or were crushed between a vehicle and a building.

The horses pulling a cart became frightened and started to run. The driver, who was walking, tried to stop them, fell, and was run over.

A man fell in the street. The wheel of a cart passed over him. He had not been drinking.

A man fell from the cart he was driving and was run over.

A child fell in front of the wheel of a three-horse cart.

An intoxicated man lying in the street at 12:30 A.M. was run over by a coach.

A fourteen-year-old girl was crushed between a cart load of bricks and the wall of a house.

A woman was sleeping in a chair at the edge of a highway. A passing cart crushed her against a lamp post.

A boy helping to pull a fire engine along a street fell and was run over by the hind wheel.

An eight-horse wagon struck a cart standing by a footpath. The tail of the cart forced the head of a female passerby against the wall of a house.

When no witness was found who could actually describe an accident involving a pedestrian, the inquisition often stated that the victim "fell" in the street and was *then* run over. Presumably this was an attempt at partial exculpation of the driver of the vehicle, whose responsibility would have been greater if his horse or vehicle had knocked down the deceased. Road accidents involving coaches often evoked many lengthy depositions. One has the impression that in such cases the possibility of manslaughter was rather carefully investigated. Perhaps these large, often rapidly moving vehicles and their horses were considered to be particularly hazardous.

Deodands were regularly reported in deaths involving horses and vehicles. When a victim was run over, the deodand was the object "moving to the death," that is, the wheel that passed over or struck the body. A wheel was customarily valued at a few shillings. The owner, and thus the person responsible for the deodand, was named in the inquisition if he was known.

When an intoxicated man riding on a dray got off, he was run over. "Verdict accy [accidentally] killed with a Deodand of 5*s*. on the Wheel."

The sum could be more. For example, a five-year-old boy was trampled and run down by a two-horse chariot; the horse was valued at £3 and the wheel at £2, clearly a punitive decision.

Horses without drivers or riders also caused fatal accidents.

A man who seized the bridle of a runaway hitched to a cart was thrown against the cart.

A man was fatally kicked by a gelding in his stall.

Analysis of the 1,907 violent deaths coming to inquest in 1780–1784 and 1805–1809 in urban and rural Shropshire revealed that 23 and 15 per cent, respectively, were caused by horses and vehicles. One-fifth of the 235 accidental deaths reported in the *Gentleman's Magazine* obituaries for 1806 had the same cause.[14] The comparable figure from the London inquisitions was 17.5 per cent (tables 3, 4). Of all fatalities involving horses, these animals when not in harness caused about one-third of the Shropshire and 19 per cent of the London (coroners' series) deaths. Of the persons killed by horses with or without vehicles, the great majority of victims in Shropshire and 80.5 per cent in London were males.[14]

Falls were responsible for 288 non-occupational accidents. Most often they occurred on ships, barges, docks, and inside houses.

A five-year-old boy and his mother were visiting the father, a carpenter, on his ship. The boy fell from the deck into the hold.

A visitor to a ship fell from the plank between it and the wharf onto the deck.

[11] (N. 3), p. 20.

[12] (N. 6.)

[13] Donald Rumbelow, *I Spy Blue* (1971, London), pp. 201–202.

[14] (N. 3), p. 9. Hair estimates the proportion of motor vehicle deaths in 1971 to have been one-fourth of all accidental deaths.

A boy fell through the skylight of a house to the pavement below.

A man leaning on the banister of a staircase in a house fell to the floor below when the banister broke.

A baby slipped from the arms of its nurse on the stairs as she stooped to pick up some bread. He fell over the banister.

There were fatal falls from windows, through trap doors, into areaways, and even on the street.

A woman sitting on a sill while she cleaned a window fell backward to the ground.

A man fell from a window during an epileptic fit.

A three-year-old boy fell out of a window.

A little girl fell through a trap door of a factory into the cellar.

A woman fell through the trap door of a shop.

A man fell through a trap door into the vault of the Church of St. Mary le Bow.

A child, taken to the top of a warehouse to see a pet monkey, fell through a loading door to the street.

A man fell in the street and struck his head.

A woman fell into the areaway of an unfinished house.

As in the case of occupational accidents, a major contributing factor was sometimes *alcohol.*

A prisoner for debt in Newgate and his visitor had several pots of beer. The visitor wished to see the prison and was shown around by his host. After two or three more pots of beer, the visitor started to leave. Both men fell down the steps; one was killed.

Several intoxicated men were boarding a Gravesend passage boat; one of them fell from the plank into the Thames.

A drunken man fell from a window.

Another fell down the stairs of a dwelling house.

An intoxicated carpenter fell. The chisel in his pocket penetrated a lung.

A drunken man trying to get into the cellar where he slept fell and struck his head on a grindstone.

A four-horse team moving at a walk struck a crate on which an intoxicated man was asleep. He fell into the street and was run over.

An American sailor fell from the window of a dwelling house while drunk.

A drunken man mixed "a certain medicine called Magnesia [and] a certain liquid call Laudanum" with gin and drank the mixture.

A beggar set fire to her clothes while intoxicated.

An intoxicated woman fell face down in the gutter and suffocated.

After drinking three half pints of brandy, four men engaged in horse-play in a small boat. Two fell into the Thames; one of these drowned.

About 2 P.M. in April, 1804, Henry Cline the younger, a well-known London surgeon, was in the operating theater of St. Thomas's Hospital when he smelled burning cloth. Entering the nearby dissecting room he found the porter who worked there unconscious and intoxicated beside the grate of the fireplace with his clothes in flames. He died five minutes later. Three hours earlier he had been seen lying drunk on the floor but three yards from the fire.

The Shropshire inquests ascribed about 10 per cent of all accidental deaths, and even more from falls from vehicles, to alcohol.[15] Drunkenness was such a common occurrence that in the London inquisitions its presence or absence was often not remarked on in cases where the context suggests the probability of intoxication.

Similarly, *darkness* in buildings and on streets seems to have been taken for granted. Pedestrians fell into unprotected areaways and cellars or were run down or crushed by passing vehicles. Many persons lost their lives when they fell into the Thames at night. Even if the splash were heard, there could be a fatal delay before a lantern was brought. When a man was heard to fall down some stairs at night, a light had to be fetched from the next house before it could be determined that he was dead. And so on.

The 243 other accidents were varied and sometimes strange. Forty people were killed by *falling objects.* A basket of sugar being lowered from a warehouse, for example, fell on a passerby when a rope broke. There were similar accidents with bundles of cork, bags of wool, a bale of flax, a bag of nails, a sack of beans, a bundle of cloth.

A wagon loaded with bales of cotton was jolted by a hole in the pavement; two bales fell off and struck a woman.

A carpenter dropped a piece of wood from the upper floor of a house; the wood struck a child.

Crushing in crowds. On February 23, 1807, a great crowd gathered in the north end of the Old Bailey[16] and in nearby streets to watch a series of executions. Some people stood on carts and others forced their way between. For a reason that was not made clear at the inquest, there was a sudden violent surge of the massed onlookers. A number of people were simply crushed; others fell and were trampled. When the crowd finally dispersed, 30 victims were stretched dead or dying on the pavement. Among them were teen-age apprentices and school boys. The father of a fourteen-year-old and the master of a young apprentice had given them permission to go to the execution. The mother of a twelve-year-old boy let him go too, but another boy of the same age attended without permission. All the boys died. A man who was crushed had taken a basket of Banbury cakes to sell to the crowd. He left a wife and four children. Of those killed, fourteen were aged sixteen or less. At least three women died in the crowd. The Court of Aldermen "appointed a Committee to look into the Melancholy Accidents."

In 1826 a beggar boy in the crowd watching another execution at the Old Bailey was crushed against a post by a wagon wheel.[17] Earlier, in 1803, a boy had

[15] Hair, 1969: p. 71.

[16] This street at that time ran in front of Newgate Prison.

[17] Public hangings at Newgate were very popular. People began

been run over by a chariot being pulled not by horses but by a noisy multitude assembled for an unspecified reason, possibly to celebrate a political victory.

A panic at the "little Theatre" in the Haymarket also took a toll. A crowd of people had waited for an hour for admission via a passage to the pit. When the door was opened, there was a rush. Someone fell on the stairs and a score or more who were following lost their footing. The people behind, not knowing what had happened, continued to push. When the passage was cleared twenty minutes later, four persons, including a mother and daughter, were dead of trampling and suffocation.

Asphyxiation in one form or another caused several fatalities. Small children visiting privies unattended fell in and suffocated. An unmarried pregnant woman who had been given a mild purgative by a surgeon reported that while seated on the privy she lost consciousness. Her baby was found suffocated in the pit. The coroner's jury accepted her story. Several babies and small children were *overlaid*, that is, while the youngster was sleeping with an older person, the latter rolled over onto the small victim, suffocating and crushing it.

An infant was overlaid by her wet nurse. A surgeon attempted unsuccessfully "to induce artificial respiration by inflating the Lungs. . . . [Overlaying] is a circumstance which not infrequently happens." The nurse did not appear to be intoxicated.

A five-months-old baby was overlaid by a twenty-months-old baby.

A tipsy mother put a baby in a bed on which were piled pieces of carpet, a fustian waistcoat, and other items. When the eight-year-old sister went to learn why the baby had not cried, she found it covered by the material.

A mother in bed with three children overlaid one of them.[18]

It is of course possible that some of the babies found dead in bed were victims of what is now known as "crib death."

Folding or "turn up" beds were deadly when an infant was placed on a bed which was later turned up by an unsuspecting child or adult.

Suffocation by burial was usually an occupational accident, but a woman who happened to be standing by a great heap of dust and ashes was buried when it collapsed. Even though a witness sought help, it was half an hour before the victim was dug out.

Charcoal fumes and the gases from a brick kiln caused a few non-occupational deaths.

to gather the night before, and by the time the execution began the next morning, crowds estimated to be as great as 40,000 had come together. Street vendors and pickpockets plied their trades. Public figures including Charles Dickens led campaigns against both capital punishment and public executions. The latter were finally abolished by Act of Parliament, the Bill passing into effect in 1868 (Anthony Babington, *The English Bastille* (London, 1971), pp. 223–227).

[18] Infanticide will be discussed in a subsequent chapter.

A large proportion of the accidental *poisoning* cases was caused by opium in various forms. Popular abuse of this drug in England in the nineteenth century occurred on a scale difficult for us to imagine. No medical authorization was required. Opiates "were as readily available as is aspirin today, and just as cheap. For a penny a man could purchase a pint of beer and, for the same sum, a quarter of an ounce of laudanum, containing about ten grains of opium."[19] Adults dosed themselves for real or imagined diseases or simply for pleasure. Various preparations in the form of syrups and cordials were widely employed to "quiet" infants and small children, particularly those left to the tender mercies of nurses by mothers who were forced to take employment away from home. Administration of the opiate was begun when the baby was a few weeks old, the dose being increased as tolerance developed. An 1843 study disclosed that in Manchester five out of six families gave laudanum to their children. One only wonders that more deaths from opium poisoning were not recorded, and indeed it is likely that many went undiscovered or were concealed.[20] If a baby or small child slowly declined for no evident reason and finally died, its demise from excessive doses of an opiate might not have been suspected; death would have been ascribed to natural causes and would not have been reported to the coroner.

A father had a bottle of laudanum to relieve headaches. During the night while sleepy he gave an overdose to his little daughter.

A mother gave a baby paregoric; "the landlady said 2 spoonfuls won't hurt it."

A twelve-year-old took some of his mother's opium pills as a lark.

A woman swallowed tincture of opium by mistake.

A woman mistook opium for the asafoetida she had been taking during a long illness.

An apprentice druggist took opium by accident.

A patient in St. Bartholomew's Hospital asked "the Night Nurse named Mary to fetch her six penny worth of Poppy to make her Sleep. Mary sayed she could not. If she did she would be turned out of her Place." But Mary later did get the patient 2*d*. worth which she bought in a shop in Aldersgate. The patient took 15 grains of the drug and died.

About 5 A.M. of a March day in 1790 a young man living in the Inner Temple rang for his manservant and laundress. They went down stairs to the bed chamber and found their master, fully dressed or nearly so and sitting by the head of the bed. In the bed was a young woman, apparently asleep. The master said, "Here's a girl who has poisoned herself. You must get some medical assistance immediately."

[19] Havard, *Homicide*, pp. 53–54. Elizabeth Lomax, "The Uses and Abuses of Opiates in Nineteenth-century England," *Bull. History Med.* **47** (1973): pp. 167–176.

[20] (N. 19), Havard, pp. 53–54. Also see discussion of infanticide in chapter VI.

The manservant returned soon with a surgeon. As was usual in cases of poisoning with an opiate—a broken bottle that had contained laudanum was seen lying in front of the fireplace—the girl was placed on her feet, dressed, and walked about the room. The surgeon then left, but sent his assistant back to the house with some medicines. About 7 A.M. the master sent his man for a second doctor, who came at once. He tried to give an emetic, but the patient could not swallow it. The first doctor returned at 10 A.M. By then the victim was clearly dying; she expired at noon.

The doctors deposed that the master had said that the girl had taken half an ounce of laudanum; the servant stated his master's estimate to have been an ounce. The master kept laudanum on hand; the servant had often purchased it for him. The doctors also deposed that the master, who seemed greatly concerned, had said at 5 A.M. that he had been giving the girl an emetic of warm water, but this had not been effective. He stated that she had taken the laudanum "out of a frolick."

The couple who kept the house where the girl lodged stated that the young man had often called for her, taken her to a tavern, and slept with her. He had repeatedly been heard by the couple to tell the girl that he would like to give her "some of the laudanum he had at home . . . [but the deponent] did not conceive at such times he was serious in what he sayed." According to one of the doctors, on the other hand, the young man asserted that the girl had often threatened to kill herself and that he had not had time to stop her from swallowing the drug.

The coroner's jury decided that the girl took the liquid "being ignorant and unaware of [its] sad and poisonous quality." The modern reader must draw his own conclusions as to whether this was accident, suicide, or homicide. In any case, the easy availability of a dangerous substance is clear.

Other victims accidentally took other poisons.

A charwoman while cleaning found in a cupboard a bottle of a liquid containing arsenic that was used to kill beetles. She drank some, supposedly thinking it was liquor. A surgeon gave an emetic and used a stomach pump but could not save her.

A child drank a vitriol solution used by a servant to clean brass.

A man died after an apothecary's assistant, who could not read or write, by mistake sold him oxalic acid instead of "Salts."

A baby drank oil of vitriol (sulphuric acid), purchased together with indigo blue to dye some baskets.

A servant took oxalic acid, kept for cleaning boot tops; he mistook the crystals for Epsom salts. Earlier he had consumed at least seven glasses of gin and some porter.

A prisoner in Newgate was troubled with ague. On the advice of his wife, he steeped an ounce of tobacco in a pint of beer as medicine. Against the advice of another prisoner, the sick man drank it all.

Two boys found a broken keg of rum. They and other passersby helped themselves to the leaking liquor with the aid of an oyster shell and a small mug. One boy died.

In 1807 the male patient of a probable quack came to grief. At the inquest, which was conducted with commendable thoroughness, it was determined that for his patient's headache, cough, and upset stomach this charlatan prescribed—the prescription itself later was found—a mixture containing half an ounce of muriatic (hydrochloric) acid, eight grains of kali (potash, potassium carbonate), five ounces of cinnamon water, and half an ounce of tincture of digitalis. Physicians who attended the dying man thought his symptoms resembled those of mercury poisoning, and the subsequent autopsy revealed inflammation and ulceration of the stomach and intestines. After the death of the patient, his servant accidentally broke the vial of medicine, spilling some on his new apron. An hour and a half later he found that holes had been burned in the garment. The individual who wrote the prescription served as parson of a Lutheran chapel and practiced physic on the side. He claimed to have attended both Guy's and St. Thomas's Hospitals as a medical student, to have attended lectures on divinity, philosophy, and medicine in Germany, and to have practiced medicine in England since 1795.

The *collapse of buildings* killed twenty-four people in non-occupational accidents. Either the structures had been damaged by fire or they simply were dilapidated through age and neglect.

Four onlookers were standing across the street from a burning house and were struck down by a falling wall.

The ruins of a house burned a day earlier fell on two boys.

Two dilapidated houses fell on a passerby.

Two adults died in the collapse of two houses under repair; the party wall had not been properly shored up.

A baby girl was killed when the roof, chimney, and upper floor of a dwelling house collapsed "from the delapidated and ruinous state and condition thereof."

It is of interest that in several of these cases the bodies of the victims were found some time later by casual passersby simply because the neighbors reported a person might be in the building. There seems to have been no organized rescue effort.

Gunpowder and firearms of course took their toll.

A man fired a musket which burst, injuring his hand. He died of a subsequent infection.

A boy found the remains of a pound of gunpowder that his father had put away in a corded box in their home. The youngster played with the powder near a fire.

When a gun was fired, a plug in the side of the barrel flew out and struck a boy in the head.

A boy shot a hen with a pistol, which burst. He "supposed he had overloaded it."

A loaded blunderbuss was discharged while being handled by a drunken man in a public house.

For an unexplained reason, someone loaded several iron swivel guns mounted on wooden carriages in Cumberland Gardens. One of them burst when fired, fatally injuring two people.

A man borrowed two spring guns because he was troubled with thieves in his barn and garden. He was told the guns were not loaded and set them in position. One was discharged; the borrower was fatally injured.

A man had difficulty removing a piece of wood from the touch hold of a gun. He therefore put the breach of the gun in his kitchen fire and at the same time put his mouth on the muzzle, intending to blow out the piece of wood. Gunpowder in the barrel exploded.

A woman held a pistol "of the value of five Shillings" against her husband and pulled the trigger. He was killed. The coroner's jury accepted her statement that she did not know the gun was loaded. However, it appeared that the deceased had been having an affair with a servant girl.

A man was shooting from his kitchen at sparrows in the yard. Laying the loaded gun on the window sill and leaning out to look for the birds, he lost his balance and fell. The gun was somehow discharged, shooting him.

A few people were killed by *animals other than horses*.

A cow broke loose and gored and tossed a child.

A bull gored a woman.

A boar used its tusks to kill its owner.

More or less accidental injuries involving *personal violence* sometimes were fatal. Some juries perhaps would have regarded these deaths as manslaughter or nonfelonious homicide.

A man running after a stage coach knocked down a sixty-nine-year-old woman.

A broken leg received in a wrestling match became fatally infected.

Two men engaged in horseplay fell to the ground. One afterward died of a ruptured bladder.

Three ragged, "very filthy" derelict boys repeatedly asked a woman for lodgings. Angry, she finally pushed one boy, who fell against another and knocked him down, fracturing his leg. The deceased, "being in a very emaciated weak and exhausted state of body from want of food and nourishment, did accelerate and occasion his death."

A man carrying a baby was accompanied by its parents. All three adults were intoxicated. A fight broke out and the man with the baby was thrown down. The baby died.

A broker and landlord came to a first-story apartment to inventory the household goods therein because the rent was overdue. Then two soldiers arrived to remove the goods to a loft nearby. When the broker attempted to have the firewood taken away, the tenant, a mother holding a nursing baby, tried to seize the wood. In the struggle the woman was pushed against a pair of double doors. They burst open and she fell out and down into the yard. The baby was killed.

A man trying to escape arrest for breach of the peace ran down the street, fell down some stairs, and struck his head.

A few deaths called accidental by a jury may well have been suicides. In such cases the jury was attempting to mitigate the shame and horror attached at the time of the taking of one's own life (see chapter VI).

A woman walking on the stone work on the outside of Blackfriars Bridge fell to the ground. The jury decided her death was accidental.

A seventeen-year-old, said to be very cheerful, had wondered "how it would feel" to be hanged. He stood on a tub in a cellar, fastened a cord around his neck and a beam, then slipped. There was no witness. The jury gave a verdict of accidental death.

Another boy died in an almost identical accident.

There was a miscellany of *unusual accidents*.

The sails of a windmill at Battersea Bank on the Thames[21] were revolving rapidly. One of them struck a servant girl on the head.

An eight-year-old boy climbing on the horsewheel[22] of a corn mill became caught in the gears and was crushed.

Two people died because they walked in their sleep and fell from the windows of upper floors.

An elderly woman slipped and fell on a chamber pot. It broke, gashing her abdomen.

A boy was looking through a key hole. Another boy on the other side, unaware of his friend, pushed a wire through the keyhole and into the first boy's eye.

A blind man was feeling his way along a street with his stick. It struck the hoof of one of three horses hitched to a cart. The team thereupon pulled the cart through a gateway and the blind man was run over.

A man was on a bed holding a bed rod. He fell off and the rod penetrated his eye.

A man was carrying a chest of drawers on his back in the street. Following behind was a boy with a Pembroke table on his head. The chest of drawers hit a clothes line stretched across the street, toppled backward, and fell on the table and the boy.

In the early nineteenth century medical men and their assistants might not feel obliged to provide emergency treatment if the patient was unable to pay.

A woman was burned when a candle ignited her clothes; "the Doctor came when he was sent for, and he looked at the deced and said it was a shocking thing and asked who was to pay him, and nobody undertaking to pay him he went away." He returned when a friend of the victim found the money.

An eighteen-month-old boy fell out of a window. He was taken to an apothecary, who "looked at the Child but said what he could do would be very expensive and this Dept [deponent] then took it to St. Bartholomew's Hospital."

Such reports, fortunately, were quite uncommon.

Over the years, increasing numbers of inquests were held in hospitals, reflecting the swelling annual totals of sick and injured patients admitted to these institutions. Aside from two inquests held at Bethlem Hospital for the insane, all took place at St. Bartholomew's in the City of London or at Guy's or St. Thomas's in Southwark. Table 5 gives details. It

[21] Perhaps close to the site of its modern successor, the Battersea Power Station.

[22] The wheel moved by the horse that supplied power.

TABLE 5

INQUESTS HELD IN HOSPITALS

	1788–1793	1794–1799	1801–1806	1807–1812	1813–1818	1819–1824	1825–1829	Total
City								
Bethlem						2		2
St. Bartholomew's	22	4	11	86	122	227	254	726
Southwark								
Guy's	1		2	22	43	99	126	293
St. Thomas's	7	1	21	55	106	154	153	497
Total	30	5	34	163	271	482	533	1518

is likely that some of the inquests reported simply as held in the Parish of St. Bartholomew the Less in the City and in the Parish of St. Thomas in Southwark actually took place in the hospitals in those parishes. If so, the totals in table 5 should be correspondingly higher. In any event, it is clear that the numbers of inquests in hospitals on victims of violence or suspected foul play increased much more rapidly than the annual numbers of all inquests. It follows that the practice of taking dangerously sick and injured people to the hospital grew steadily between 1788 and 1829, particularly after the turn of the century.

A review of the numbers of occupational and non-occupational accidents by cause and period (table 4) is instructive. As already mentioned, during a time when London's population approximately doubled, deaths from burns increased more than sevenfold. Drownings remained at about the same level, finally declining in 1824–1829. Falls almost tripled. Deaths involving vehicles and horses kept pace with the population growth. Collectively, all other accidents tripled. Probably the increasing mechanization of the Industrial Revolution was a factor.

The striking disproportion in the numbers of male (2,529) and female (773) accidental deaths (table 3) is only partly accounted for by the fact that most employed persons were males. Of the non-occupational deaths, 67.3 per cent were male, 32.1 per cent were female, and the remainder were of unspecified sex. Males were in the streets in greater numbers, and boys certainly have always had a greater propensity for getting into dangerous situations than have girls. Only burns, particularly those received at home, caused more female than male deaths. Hair makes a similar observation for the Shropshire inquests.[23] In metropolitan London in 1840, 60.3 per cent of the victims of burns and scalds were female.[24]

TABLE 6

ACCIDENTS BY AGE GROUP AND SEX

	Male	Female	Unknown	Total
Infant (under 2 years)	176	138	1	315
Child (under 14 years)	429	207	3	639
Adult	1392	339	1	1732
Not stated	532	89	9	629
	2529	773	14	3316

Analysis of the distribution of accidents by age can only be approximate, since age often was not specified in the depositions and inquisitions. When I felt justified by the context, I categorized an accident victim as an infant (under two years), child (under fourteen years), or adult. For example, a female in its mother's arms would be counted as an infant, while a mariner would be considered an adult. Categorization was complicated by popular and legal usage of "infant" to include children. The age of many victims could not be determined at all. Thus the data in table 6 must be regarded with caution.

If the totals for each age group are considered in relation to the number of years of life for each group, i.e., the first two years as an infant, the next twelve as a child, and the next forty or so as an adult, it is clear that the size of the groups is not proportional to the span of years and that, relatively, even when allowance is made for the smaller numbers of people who were at risk in the older age groups, it was most dangerous to be an infant, less so a child, and least of all an adult. In metropolitan London in 1840, 38 per cent of the male and 51.5 per cent of the female deaths from violence (except suicide) occurred in persons under twenty years of age.[25]

Table 7 shows the distribution of male accidents by month. In this and other tables giving distribution of deaths by month, 1788 and 1829 are omitted because some inquisitions were missing for these years. The total of 151 cases for February is exceptional because 25 of the 30 persons who were crushed in the crowd watching executions in February, 1807 (see page 26), were males. Except for February, 1807, there were no more than 15 male accidental deaths in any one month of one year; the overall monthly average was 5.4. Clearly the lowest proportion was in February and March and the highest in July and August.

As with occupational accidents, many persons dying after non-occupational injuries such as lacera-

[23] (N. 15), p. 70.
[24] (N. 3), p. 211.
[25] (N. 4), p. 233.

tions and compound fractures succumbed not to the primary injury, often in itself not life-threatening, but to the infection—"mortification" or "erysipelas"—that developed a few days later.

V. DEATHS FROM ILLNESS

The coroner was concerned with deaths from illness if they occurred suddenly, or in circumstances which appeared or were reported to be suspicious, or in prison. In the 1,263 inquisitions on deaths of prisoners from all causes, 1,056 male and 171 female deaths were ascribed to illness and the remainder, 36, to accident, suicide, and homicide. Table 8 analyzes the reported "causes" of death from illness of a sample of 607 prisoners. The reported causes, of course, have several kinds of deficiencies when viewed against the background of twentieth-century medicine. Many terms are inexact. Some, e.g., dropsy, convulsions, refer to symptoms rather than diseases. Not all diagnoses were made by medical men; even if they were, usually there had been no autopsy. Finally, the medical knowledge available was at its best that of a century and a half to two centuries ago.

Fever and chills were allegedly the leading causes of death by illness. How often these were manifestations of the dread jail fever (epidemic typhus), we cannot tell. The disease had taken a heavy toll earlier in the eighteenth century and was still a hazard in the nineteenth. Epidemic typhus was and is carried by lice. The filth and overcrowding that characterized most prisons of course facilitated the spread of typhus and many other diseases. Dr. John Hunter[1] had shown in 1779 that "gaol fever" was the same disease as that well known in the crowded areas of large cities and in workhouses and hospitals.[2] John Howard, the great prison reformer, wrote in 1780[3] that

> what terrifies most of us from looking into prisons, is the gaol distemper so frequent in them.
>
> . . . .
>
> From my own observations in 1773 and 1774, I was fully

[1] Not to be confused with Mr. John Hunter the surgeon, anatomist, and experimental biologist.

[2] Charles Creighton, *A History of Epidemics in Britain* (London, 1965) **2**: pp. 91, 134, 138. Babington, *English Bastille*, pp. 8, 97–98, 105.

[3] John Howard, *The State of the Prisons in England and Wales* (Warrington, 1780), pp. 2, 11, 431.

TABLE 7

MALE ACCIDENTS BY MONTH

Jan.	198	July	251
Feb.	151	Aug.	245
Mar.	166	Sept.	231
April	188	Oct.	218
May	178	Nov.	205
June	182	Dec.	214
			2527

TABLE 8

DEATHS FROM ILLNESS IN PRISON BY "CAUSE" AND SEX

	Male	Female	Total
Fever, chills	204	26	233
Age, natural death	96	18	114
Decline, decay	53	19	72
Consumption	45	2	47
Asthma, shortness of breath	21		21
Bowel complaint, flux, vomiting	15	4	19
Dropsy	13	2	15
Smallpox	11		11
Not stated	9		9
Convulsions, palsy, St. Vitus' dance	6	4	10
Hunger, exposure	5		5
Stomach complaint	5		5
Apoplexy	4	1	5
Gravel, stone	4		4
Head complaint, brain fever	4		4
Inward complaint, stoppage	4	2	6
Chest disease, lung disease	3	1	4
Cough, cold	3	3	6
Mortification	3		3
Scurvy	3		3
Venereal complaint	3	2	5
Deranged	2		2
Jaundice	2		2
Gout	1		1
Cancer		1	1
Total	522	85	607

> convinced that many more were destroyed by it [jail fever], than were put to death by all the public executions in the kingdom.
>
> . . . .
>
> Convicts . . . are ironed, and thrust into close offensive dungeons, some of them without straw or other bedding; in which they continue, in winter, sixteen or eighteen hours out of the twenty-four, in utter inactivity, and immersed in the noxious effluvia of their own bodies.

Since typhus was really endemic, it may well have been responsible for most of the deaths ascribed to chills and fever.

Coroners had been obliged since medieval times to hold an inquest on every death that occurred in prison.[4] Umfreville specified in 1761[5] that

> in the Case of a *Prisoner's* dying in Gaol it is the Office or Duty of the Gaoler to send for the Coroner, to inquire how the Deceased came by his Death; the better to remove a possible Presumption, that the Prisoner died "*per dure Gard*," the ill Usage or Severity of his Gaoler, and it may be presumed a public Officer may be privately Guilty, who denies or neglects a public Inquiry.

Nearly all prisoners reportedly died of natural causes. In such cases the verdict of the coroner's jury was "natural death by the visitation of God." This formula had come down from the *ex visitatione divina* or *ex visitatione Dei* of Elizabethan[6] and earlier days. It neatly avoided the assumption of official liability,

[4] Hunnisett, *Medieval Coroner*, pp. 35–36.

[5] Umfreville, *Lex coronatoria*, pp. 209–210, 489.

[6] T. R. Forbes, "London Coroners' Inquests for 1590."

first by making clear that the victim had been ill—the usual verdict, "natural causes," being as irrefutable as it was nonspecific—and second by attributing death to divine intervention. Who could argue with this?

The phrase "by the visitation of God" was, however, to bring down the wrath of nineteenth-century critics of the coroner system. An editorial in the March 28, 1874, issue of the *Lancet* struck out at this "verdict which ought not to be allowed."[7] The editorial was inspired in part by a recent controversy in the town of Whitby, where the medical officer of health had criticized the town coroner for allowing his jury to employ the useless and imprecise phrase. The medical officer quoted the Registrar General's report for 1841:

> To the question, "What is the cause of death?" such verdicts as Natural death or Visitation of God, it is scarcely necessary to say, are no answers at all, but mere evasions of the inquiry.

The Whitby coroner was offended, stating that

> He considered it a piece of impertinence for any medical man to make such remarks upon the verdicts of juries, and especially so when the inquiries were held by an experienced coroner and a lawyer of long standing. It would never do to allow individual medical men to set up their *ipse dixit* against the law of the land . . . To such medical men he would say, "Mind your own business."

As for the verdict, "Died by the visitation of God," observed the coroner,

> He was happy to say he had not yet outlived his belief in God, and he hoped it would be long before an English jury could be found that had done so.

Age, natural death, decline, and decay tell us little about actual causes. When deaths were ascribed to hunger and exposure, the victims were dead or dying vagrants picked up in the streets, usually by watchmen.

A homeless man expired in Poultry Compter "being ill and diseased, for want of sufficient Necessaries and for want of proper care and attention."

A woman arrested in the street because she seemed drunk died during the night in Poultry Compter.

A watchman saw a wet and dirty man sitting at the door of a house about 5 A.M. Asked his business, he said he was cold. At 7:30 A.M. he was found dead in the same doorway. A surgeon at St. Thomas's Hospital said the man had "died from the inclemency of the weather."

A beadle taking his turn as constable of the night was sent to the Custom House Quay, where he found a drunken man insensible in a chair. He was carried to the watch house and medical help was sent for. In the morning the man was taken to the workhouse; he died the next day.

A vagrant was ultimately the responsibility of the parish of his or her origin. If arrested and convicted, he served his sentence, then was returned by the authorities to his own parish.

A man who died in the Bridewell Hospital had been "adjudged . . . to be a Rogue and Vagabond to be kept and set to hard Labour for seven days and then to be passed by due course of Law" to his place of origin.

Sometimes neglect or callousness on the part of the watch appears to have contributed to a death.

An emaciated, dirty woman was found sitting on a tub in a privy by a constable. Because she could not give a good account of herself and he suspected she had stolen the tub, he took her to the Giltspur Street Compter. From there she was sent, although she "appeared Cold and ill," to the Guildhall, accompanied by a jailer. On the way she collapsed, was picked up, and after a few steps fell again. The jailer then went for a coach, but she died in a few minutes.

A man accused of stealing the sheets and pillow slip from his bed by a landlord was confined in the watch house on a felony charge. He cut his throat with a pen knife. The watch house keeper said he had previously searched the prisoner. The verdict of the coroner's jury was suicide while lunatic.

A coroner's jury decided that a man died "from excessive drinking and the inclemency of the weather" and that the officers of the watch had accelerated his death by leaving him "in an Engine House without covering or fire" from 2:30 P.M. on 24 December to 9 A.M. 25 December.

A watchman found a man lying on the foot pavement with his head resting on his hat, shoes, and wig. He "was very dirty and his right eye appeared to be much hurt and bled a good deal." The man was taken to the watch house, covered with a great coat, and allowed to remain all night. The next morning he was turned out at the door, still unable to tell the watch where he lived. A little later an innkeeper found him speechless on the pavement. The innkeeper opened the watch house door and asked that the victim be put in front of the fire until help could be brought from the parish. However, the watchman refused, saying he was going off duty and the house would be closed. The innkeeper then got the parish beadle. The latter said he could not admit the victim to the poor house without an order from a parish officer. The innkeeper again requested admission of the unconscious man to the watch house, "observing that the beadle would take care of the key until Dept [deponent, the innkeeper] could procure an order from one of the Officers of the parish for the deced to be received into the poor house." The watchman again refused. Finally an officer of the parish was found; he ordered the victim taken by the beadle to the poor house. There the man died.

Thus we see outlined the mechanics for dealing with a not uncommon parish problem. In all fairness, such a degree of inertia on the part of petty officials seems to have been exceptional.

---

[7] "Death by 'the visitation of God,' " *Lancet* 1: p. 452.

Most of the other causes of death in table 8 are self-explanatory. Gravel and stone were concretions in the urinary tract. Mortification, it will be recalled, referred to gangrene. People did not die because they were deranged or had gout, but these conditions could coincide with a disease that was fatal.

As already noted, existence in the prisons was crowded and filthy almost beyond belief for those who could not pay for better accommodations. Many writers have described the dreadful quarters in which men and women had to try to survive.[8] Infrequently the depositions also give a hint.

An asthmatic male who died in the Fleet Prison had been confined for some days in the Strong Room, "a very close Room and below the Surface of the Ground and the flooring of it stoned."

The inquisitions and depositions on prison deaths nearly always emphasize that the sick prisoner was "regularly attended" by a surgeon, his assistant, or an apothecary, but there are few details. Howard's great survey of London prisons indicates that in half of them the post of surgeon was not filled.[9]

Although this author makes several references to children in prison,[10] I found no mention of inquests on deaths of such children. Ages of prisoners who died were seldom stated; it is of course possible that some of them were not adults.

One man expired in prison as a result of a bullet wound received nearly three months earlier. While breaking into a house at about two in the morning, he had been discovered and shot with a pistol by the householder.

There were a few noblemen in prison. From June 2 to 8, 1780, at the height of agitation against the Roman Catholics, London was shaken by the Gordon Riots, or No-Popery Riots, led by Lord George Gordon (1751–1793). The Fleet Prison was burned down, Newgate Prison was stormed and sacked, and all the other prisons were opened. More than 450 people were killed and wounded. In the following years Lord Gordon was intermittently in trouble and finally, in January, 1788, was sentenced to five years in Newgate. At the end of his term, since he was unable to post security for good behavior, his confinement was continued. He died in Newgate on November 1, 1793, after an illness of two weeks.[11]

His inquest was held at nine on the morning of Saturday, November 2, in the prison. A woman servant of Gordon deposed that two weeks earlier he had shivered, complained of cold, and lost his appetite. He was attended in his last illness, she said, by an apothecary and by Dr. Lettsom, a physician. The inquisition is missing; the endorsement on the single deposition says that Lord George died a natural death. Timbs states that death was due to the gaol distemper.[12]

It is probable that a good many of the inquisitions and depositions on deaths in prison are not included in the series at the Records Office. Between 1789, the first complete year, and 1828, the last complete year, of this series, the annual total of prisoners' deaths for which records are present varies from an unexplained high of 119 in 1789 to a low of 5 in 1822. The average is 30. The totals by prison appear in table 1.

A tabulation by Colquhoun shows that 2,788 individuals were discharged from the eight prisons in the London area in one year ending in October, 1795.[13] However, in attempting to establish prison mortality rates one should consider the annual number of deaths in relation not to the numbers of prisoners admitted or discharged per year but to the average prison population. In the first half of the nineteenth century, if an individual were sent to prison for his felony (instead of receiving a sentence of execution or of transportation for seven years, fourteen years, or life), his term, at least, was relatively short. In 1854 the average period of detention in English and Welsh prisons was only forty-eight days.[14] Any attempt to develop a mortality rate is further complicated by factors of age, increasing susceptibility to disease as confinement continues, and so on. Unfortunately the present study does not provide the data necessary to establish actual mortality rates. However, some measure of the threat to health resulting from incarceration is indicated by a conclusion drawn from a study of deaths in 1825–1842 in London's then new, model Millbank Penitentiary: "The criminal's liability to die was more than doubled by imprisonment."[15]

Now let us consider the inquests on death from illness that did *not* occur in prison (table 9). Once again, natural death and *age* were leading "causes." Apoplexy was frequently invoked, although this verdict was often rendered in the absence of a post-mortem examination. Excessive drinking was a significant cause of death. The intake of alcohol in some cases was startling, even in an age notable for the consumption of drink.

A man consumed three half pints of gin in twenty minutes.

A man died "in consequence of excessive drinking of new Rum."

A man, already intoxicated, drank part of a pint of gin and collapsed.

---

[8] See, for example (N. 3). Also, M. C. Buer, *Health, Wealth, and Population in the Early Days of the Industrial Revolution* (New York, 1968), pp. 195–196.

[9] (N. 3), Howard, p. 173 *et seq.*

[10] (N. 3), Howard, pp. 10, 46, 179, 187, 189, 212.

[11] (N. 2), Babington, pp. 14, 120–122.

[12] John Timbs, *Curiosities of London* (1867, London), p. 698. John C. Lettsom (1744–1815), L.R.C.P., F.S.A., F.R.S., was a distinguished Quaker physician and philanthropist of London.

[13] [P. Colquhoun], *A Treatise on the Police of London* (1798, Philadelphia), p. 179.

[14] McCulloch, *Account of the British Empire*, p. 566.

[15] (N. 14), pp. 565–568.

TABLE 9

DEATHS FROM ILLNESS NOT IN PRISON BY "CAUSE" AND SEX

	Male	Female	Total
Age, natural death	286	112	398
Apoplexy	54	22	76
Excessive drinking	44	14	58
Consumption	15	6	21
Suddenly	14	8	22
Starvation, exposure	13	3	16
Brain disease	8	4	12
Killed self in delirium	8	3	11
Heart disease	6	2	8
Aneurysm (except apoplexy)	5	4	9
Fever	4		4
Inflammation	4		4
Decline, long sick	3		3
Convulsions	2	3	5
Internal disease	2	4	6
Stomach disease	2	2	4
Erysipelas	1		1
Fit	1		1
Rupture	1		1
Smallpox	1		1
Land scurvy		2	2
Miscarriage		2	2
Not stated		2	2
Uterine disease		2	2
Epilepsy		1	1
Liver disease		1	1
Measles		1	1
Prematurity		1	1
Venereal disease		1	1
Whooping cough		1	1
Total	474	201	675

A man drank a pint of gin without stopping.

A man drank an excess of whisky from a cask on a quay.

A laborer collapsed ten minutes after he was seen drinking from a pail of brandy dregs in a warehouse.

A woman died from an excess of rum.

While playing skittles, a man had three glasses of gin and water; on his way home he added a two-penny glass of gin.

On an unidentified, unconscious man was found "a small tube such as a person might take Spirits by from Casks."

A ship's boy got very drunk, then had nearly a pint of whisky.

To win a wager, a man drank a quart of gin in five minutes. The bystanders confirmed his achievement. In three or four minutes he fell from his chair.

A laborer came into an alehouse about 6:30 A.M. and had a half pint of beer with a penny's worth of gin, then a half pint of an unspecified beverage, then a half pint of gin, then a half pint of rum. "Soon afterward the deced became speechless."

Mention has earlier been made of vagrants suffering from exposure who were picked up by the watch and died in jail. Other unfortunates were found by passers-by.

A man died after being "exposed to the Inclemency of the Weather in the open Air in Fleet Market" from two until nine of a January morning.

An intoxicated man wandered about the streets during all the night of Christmas Day.

A seventy-seven-year-old woman died of cold in her room in January.

A beggar was found dead of cold in the road in March. An autopsy showed emaciation and "general disease throughout his whole frame."

A diseased and intoxicated man died of exposure at the end of December.

The deaths of persons who killed themselves while delirious could, presumably, be categorized as due to illness, accident, or even suicide while of unsound mind. None of these designations is really satisfactory. I have included these deaths with those due to natural causes, that being the verdict of the jury.

Land scurvy was an old name for what we call *purpura*.

Table 10 shows the distribution by month of 927 male and 275 female deaths from illness, both in and out of prison. Perhaps partly because the number of female deaths is relatively small, their seasonal trend, if any, is not apparent. The totals for males, however, show a reasonably smooth progression between a high in January and a low in July, suggesting a correlation between the cold months and increased deaths from fatal illness that came to inquest.

Puzzling to coroners' juries in the past, as they are today, were the deaths of some individuals who expired not long after both a serious injury and an illness. Which was the actual cause? I have in all instances categorized such deaths according to the verdicts of the juries. When an injury was followed by an overwhelming infection or "mortification" (see chapters on accidents), the situation usually appeared to be clear cut, the illness being secondary to the injury. Sometimes it was suspected that a fatal illness resulted from maltreatment.

Although a man was observed by his wife to be incoherent and behaving strangely, he was allowed to enlist in the army. After an unspecified episode, he was taken in handcuffs by a sergeant and a private on the Maidstone coach. He resisted getting out of the coach. Observers said his eyes were discolored and his face and ears were scratched. The sergeant was observed to threaten but not to strike him. The man became physically ill, was taken to the poor house, and was seen by a surgeon. The prisoner at that time had black eyes and bruises, could not speak, was

TABLE 10

MALE AND FEMALE ILLNESS BY MONTH, 1789–1828

	Male	Female		Male	Female
Jan.	117	26	July	48	17
Feb.	87	21	Aug.	59	34
Mar.	87	22	Sep.	63	22
Apr.	75	26	Oct.	70	21
May	74	14	Nov.	82	32
June	53	15	Dec.	112	25
				927	275

delirious and uncomprehending, and seemed to have "a low typhus fever." He died in a fortnight. After death the body was opened. No marks of external violence were reported but there was distention of the cerebral vessels and "a slight effusion of bloody water in the cavity of the Scull." Death was ascribed to typhus.

An unidentified woman, recently widowed, came to England from Cuba in 1806. She was put in a prison ship at Chatham, presumably because of her alien status. Then she was turned over to a merchant so that he could send her "back to Spain." However, her violent behavior and attempts at suicide led to a medical diagnosis of insanity and in September, 1807, she was placed in a private "House for Lunatics," the merchant paying for her care. The woman who operated the asylum and her servant deposed that the deranged woman was well cared for, was kept in a room with a board floor, had a fire in cold weather, and never had irons put on her limbs. However, early in 1811 she complained of sores on her ankle and was taken to St. Bartholomew's Hospital, where she died about three weeks later of a mortification of her leg. James Parkinson, the London surgeon[16] who had cared for her, deposed that she had been insane three years earlier, had partially recovered, but had refused to leave the asylum. He said death was due to the mortification. The verdict was natural death.

There were inquests on deaths of apprentices and servants as a result of the abuse of a master or mistress. Sometimes a verdict of homicide was returned (see next chapter). In other cases, the jury was obviously suspicious, examining a large number of witnesses at length, but felt obliged to reach a verdict of natural death.

An eleven-year-old girl was apprenticed by her parish, together with two other girls, to learn the trade of pin-heading.[17] One of the surviving girls deposed that they were well treated by their master, a bookbinder, and mistress until the parish had paid the apprentice fee at the end of the first nine weeks. Thereafter the girls were stripped naked and beaten with a birch rod or a piece of wood by a journey woman when they did not meet their hourly production rate or spoiled their work. The beatings were ordered by the mistress, who was lying in. The eleven-year-old was beaten on the body and head with a file until it broke. She was in addition at various times, kicked, stamped, struck with the handle of a hammer, etc. The master also kicked and beat her. The girls, who were poorly fed, began work at six in the morning and stopped at eleven at night. After several months the eleven-year-old girl became fatally ill. She was then seen by Mr. John Wilson and Mr. Thomas Smart, surgeons, who decided her condition was due to consumption. After her death, the body was opened by these men and Sir William Blizard.[18] They found "slight" bruises on the scalp, an abnormal amount of fluid in the ventricles of the brain, an abscess and tubercles in the lungs, a polyp in the right auricle of the heart, and extreme emaciation. Death was ascribed to disease, the surgeons conceding that they could not find signs of fatal violence. They added that "hard labour and ill usage" might have accelerated the death.

The autopsy of a servant girl revealed two quarts of water in the chest, pericardial adhesions, disease of the liver, stomach, and intestines, and a laceration on the forehead. Both signed and anonymous letters, evidently introduced at the inquest, claimed that the girl died as the result of savage beatings by her master. The coroner's jury returned a verdict of natural death.

An eleven-year-old girl was one of thirty apprentices to a lace maker. When admitted to Guy's Hospital she was dirty, verminous, debilitated, ravenous, and ulcerated. Autopsy disclosed an external ulcer communicating with diseased vertebrae. "The Viscera of the body was [*sic*] healthy and there was no glandular disease." The verdict was "natural death by the visitation of God."

The deaths of "battered children" injured in their homes were investigated at inquests. Again the numerous and lengthy depositions strongly suggest the sympathy and shock of the witnesses and the court, but the juries returned verdicts of natural death.

A woman was seen to strike her four-year-old nurse child[19] on the head with her fist and then to hold the child's hair with one hand and beat him on various parts of the body with her other hand. She then sat the little boy on a table. He cried, fell back, stretched, and did not move again. A surgeon found a bruise on the left ear but judged it did not indicate a serious injury. He said the child would not have cried if it had received a fatal blow on the head. The verdict was natural death.

A woman put her head out of the window of a house and screamed, "For God sake come up for my Husband will murder my Child." Passers-by rushed into the house and found her holding a four-week-old baby boy. His face was black. He was taken to an apothecary, who "said it was in a dying state long before then and desired her to take it back again." Soon after the baby died. The coroner's jury decided death was due to natural causes.

Several sick or pregnant women may have died as a result of violence done to them, but again the juries gave verdicts of "natural death by the visitation of God."

An intoxicated woman in late pregnancy was pushed off a stool, fell to the floor, and died of a hemorrhage.

A crowd of Irishmen broke into a shop and man-

---

[16] Parkinson (1755–1824), a student of John Hunter, is best known for his classic description (1817) of paralysis agitans, Parkinson's disease. He also published the first report in English of a case of appendicitis.

[17] Fitting heads on pins, once a stage in their manufacture.

[18] Blizard (1743–1835) was surgeon to the London Hospital and helped to found a medical school there. He was twice president of the Royal College of Surgeons.

[19] Foster child.

handled the shopkeeper and his pregnant wife. She miscarried and had a fatal hemorrhage.

A woman under treatment for land scurvy was beaten by her husband. She died two weeks later in St. Bartholomew's Hospital. An autopsy disclosed ulceration of the large intestine, an effusion of blood, and bruises. The surgeon did not think there was evidence that the beating had been fatal.

The body of a naked woman, seventy to eighty years old, was found in a basket in a causeway near the Thames. She had a "mortal" skull fracture. However, at autopsy pus was found under the fracture "which could not have taken place unless the injury was sustained during life." This was a rare case in which the jury reached no verdict.

Sometimes persons who died after being in a fight were judged to have succumbed to natural causes, as in the following instances.

Two prisoners, allegedly friends, in Newgate had a fist fight over ownership of some basil strings,[20] according to the suspiciously identical depositions of three other prisoners. In the fight, one prisoner was pushed to the pavement, got up, fell forward, striking his forehead, and died. A surgeon, who clearly did a careful autopsy, deposed that he found no external marks of violence except a small bruise on the forehead. When the head was opened, no signs of fatal injury were found.

A woman who often fought with her husband died. A surgeon found no external signs of violence. When the skull was opened, 10–12 ounces of blood were found in the ventricles. The surgeon said that death had been caused by this hemorrhage, but he could not determine whether the latter was due to injury or to apoplexy.

A man became ill after being struck on the head with a fist in a fight. An autopsy was performed by Thomas Clarke and Sir Astley Cooper.[21] Nothing was found that the surgeons felt they could ascribe to external violence, but they did observe abnormal amounts of pericardial and subarachnoid fluid.

A ship's apprentice, in a fight on a fishing smack, was punched in the face and fell overboard, striking a vessel alongside. When rescued, he vomited blood. Autopsy revealed no injuries.

A woman in late pregnancy flew into a rage, attacked another woman, collapsed, and died in four or five minutes. Autopsy showed massive intrathoracic and intrapericardial hemorrhage.

Alternatively, in some inquests that disclosed both illness and a serious injury, the jury decided that death was due to the latter. In such a case, the jury had to try to determine whether the injury was accidental or deliberate (see next chapter).

[20] Strings used to suspend the chains of basils, or ankle fetters, so that walking would be somewhat less difficult.

[21] Astley Paston Cooper (1768–1841) was one of the most distinguished surgeons and anatomists of the period. He made significant contributions on a variety of subjects including hernias, fractures, dislocations, and the anatomy of the breast.

VI. SUICIDES AND HOMICIDES

The 6,351 inquisitions include 658 on the deaths of males and 283 on the deaths of females judged to have committed suicide. The methods of suicide are listed in table 11. Hanging was the choice for almost half of both sexes. These individuals used a rope, cord, handkerchief, or similar object of, according to the deodands, little or no value. Stabbing and cutting with a knife, razor, or shears, again usually of small value, was the next most frequent method, being elected more frequently by males than females. One in eight of the males, but none of the females, chose shooting. A pistol was almost always employed.

Poison was chosen by a greater proportion of women than men. Often the agent was laudanum; as mentioned in a previous chapter, this drug was cheap and easily available. Arsenic in various forms was readily acquired; one victim drank "bug water" purchased for its arsenic content from a greengrocer. A few of the surgeons called to treat such patients or to perform autopsies did chemical tests on vomitus or stomach contents to identify the poison.

Jumping from a height was, like poison, preferred by a greater proportion of women than men. Only 32 persons who drowned themselves were recorded as suicides but, as previously noted, it seems likely that many drowning deaths categorized by the juries as accidental were actually deliberate. One deranged woman choked herself with two garters and two handkerchiefs and another disturbed woman tore open an abdominal hernia, eviscerating herself.

Analysis of 851 suicides by month (table 12) showed totals ranging from high points in February and May to a low point in November. The reasons for the differences are not clear.

As Hair[1] points out, most, if not all, suicide statistics are suspect because there is good reason to believe that not all suicides are reported. Hence we must approach the data with caution. In Tudor times suicides, according to one study, constituted 21 per cent of all deaths by suicide and misadventure.[2] Farr's analysis of the Bills of Mortality[3] indicates that the proportion of suicides to all violent deaths increased from 8.5 per cent in 1647–1700 to 18.6 per cent in 1800–1829, but the violent deaths included a large number of executions. If the latter are excluded, the corrected percentages are 9.8 per cent for 1647–1700 and 12.2 per cent for 1800–1829. Hair's study[4] of violent deaths in Shropshire reveals that suicides ranged from 11 per cent of the total in 1785–1789 to 7 per cent in 1805–1809. Two-thirds of those known to have committed suicide were males. In 1840 in

[1] Hair, "Deaths from Violence in Britain: A Tentative Secular Survey."

[2] P. E. H. Hair, "A Note on the Incidence of Tudor Suicide," *Local Pop. Studies* #5 (1970): pp. 36–43.

[3] Farr, *Statistics*, p. 288.

[4] Hair, "Accidental Death and Suicide in Shropshire, 1780–1809," pp. 63–75.

London, suicides constituted 15.5 per cent of all violent deaths; again, two-thirds were those of males. In England in 1840 male suicide was most frequently by hanging, followed in order by cutting and stabbing, poison, drowning, and shooting. For females, hanging again was the most usual method, followed by poisoning, drowning, and cutting and stabbing.[5] In Greater London in 1972 there were 3,035 deaths from violent causes; of these, 718, or 23.7 per cent, were reported as suicides. Of the suicides, 53.5 per cent were female.[6]

Not only are suicide statistics for past centuries unreliable, but the proportions of suicides to all violent deaths are affected by the rise and fall in numbers of accidental deaths. Thus one cannot with confidence compare the percentage of suicides in one historical period with that in another.

Although by the late eighteenth century less stigma was attached to suicide than, for example, in Elizabethan times,[7] deliberate self-destruction was still looked on as a wicked and shameful act. Hence it was the usual practice, as it had been for centuries, for a coroner's jury to specify in the inquisition for a suicide that the individual acted while "not being of sound Mind, Memory and Understanding but lunatic and distracted."[8] If the suicide victim was mentally ill when he destroyed himself, then clearly he was not responsible for his action and no shame should attach to it. In addition, in this case he had not committed a felony and his property was not forfeit to the Crown.

It was frequently deposed at the inquest on a suicide that the deceased had been depressed.

A clerk who took laudanum had had financial troubles and had quarreled with his wife. She left him.

A man who shot himself was about to be arrested for debt.

A man who jumped from a window at the top of a house had been in ill health, "complained his head was bad," and was sometimes deranged.

A mattress maker who cut his throat had "fits of Melancholy."

A woman who destroyed herself had a history of melancholia and had been for five or six weeks in a madhouse.

A woman poisoned herself after the man who had "paid her addresses" for the past year told her he had just married someone else.

A man who cut his throat had had a "brain fever" two years earlier and had since been deranged.

TABLE 11

SUICIDES BY METHOD AND SEX

	Male (%)	Female (%)	Total (%)
Hanging	314 (47.8)	140 (49.5)	455 (48.3)
Stabbing, cutting	186 (28.2)	54 (19.1)	240 (25.5)
Shooting	83 (12.6)		83 (8.8)
Poison	43 (6.5)	44 (15.5)	87 (9.2)
Jumping from height	18 (2.7)	25 (8.8)	43 (4.6)
Drowning	14 (2.1)	18 (6.4)	32 (3.4)
Choking		1 (0.4)	1 (0.1)
Evisceration		1 (0.4)	1 (0.1)
	658	283	941

There were additional cases, as we have seen, in which an individual took his own life during delirium.

Most suicides were carried out at home, in a bedroom or privy, or at the place of employment, usually behind a locked door. However, a few suicides occurred in public buildings.

The parish clerk of a church hanged himself from a bannister of the gallery of his church.

A prisoner arrested for violent behavior, including an attack on a member of the patrol, cut his throat with an unspecified sharp object in the watch house.

A patient at Bethlehem Hospital who was considered incurably insane was locked in her cell without clothes or sheets. In the morning she was found hanged with a silk handkerchief.

A deranged patient at St. Thomas's Hospital threw himself from a window.

A number of individuals committing suicide were unwilling to rely on a single method and used, or were prepared to use, two lethal methods.

A man cut his throat after drinking a liquid containing opium and arsenic. In his room were found two loaded pistols.

Two individuals each shot themselves with two pistols.

TABLE 12

MALE AND FEMALE SUICIDES AND HOMICIDES BY MONTH, 1789–1828

	Suicides		Homicides	
	Number	Per cent	Number	Per cent
Jan.	69	8.1	13	9.9
Feb.	84	9.9	11	8.4
Mar.	71	8.3	15	11.5
Apr.	76	8.9	10	7.6
May	84	9.9	7	5.3
June	64	7.5	9	6.9
July	72	8.5	16	12.2
Aug.	79	9.3	9	6.9
Sept.	67	7.9	11	8.4
Oct.	74	8.7	7	5.3
Nov.	52	6.1	12	9.2
Dec.	59	6.9	11	8.4
	851		131	

[5] *Report of the Registrar General* (1845), pp. 252–257.

[6] *Registrar General's Statistical Review* (1974), p. 309.

[7] Forbes, *Chronicle*, pp. 165–168. The sample form recommended to magistrates by Umfreville for a warrant to bury a *felo de se*, one who had "feloniously, wilfully, and of his Malice [a]forethought, killed and murdered himself," was addressed to the church wardens and constables of the parish and directed them, in part, "to cause the Body of the said A.B. to be buried in some public Highway." The document admonished parish officers that "in this case your Warrant is not to be directed to the Minister, for no Service is to be said." (Umfreville, *Lex coronatoria*, pp. 498–499.)

[8] (N. 7), Umfreville, pp. 310–311.

A man employed in a chemist's shop cut his throat. Autopsy disclosed sulphuric ether in his stomach.

At least three persons committing suicide were teenagers; it is possible that there were others whose youthful age was not revealed.

A fifteen-year-old mentally disturbed girl poisoned herself after her theft of eight sovereigns from her master was detected.

An errand boy to a hatter hanged himself.

An apprentice to a coffin plate manufacturer was found hanged. Both boys were described as "cheerful."

When a jury was disposed to be lenient, the suicidal nature of a death could be concealed.

A woman who had been "dull and melancholy . . . accidentally choaked and strangled [herself] by a Garter which she had round her Neck." The verdict was accidental death.

An autopsy on a girl, a chronic alcoholic, disclosed damage, apparently by a corrosive poison, to the lining of the esophagus and stomach. The verdict was natural death.

A man who was said to have been depressed hanged himself with a cord. The verdict was accidental death.

On the other hand, as indicated in table 2, fifteen males and one female were found by coroners' juries to have committed suicide but the merciful notation that the victims were "lunatic" was withheld. Instead, each inquisition included the charge, as specified also in Umfreville,[9] that the deceased,

> not having the Fear of God before his eyes, but being moved and seduced by the Instigation of the Devil . . . with Force and Arms . . . in and upon himself in the Peace of God and of our said Sovereign Lord the King, then and there feloniously, wilfully and of his Malice aforethought, did make an Assault . . . did kill and murder himself. . . .

Except for the identification of the victim, this was also the formula used for a homicide. Here was unleashed the full outrage of the law at the taking of human life. Further, since suicide in this case was a felony, the property of the *felo de se* was forfeit.

Of course we ask, why did coroners' juries in some cases withhold the mitigating formula of suicide while of unsound mind? For four of the sixteen victims, there was no clue. One of these deaths was that of the coffin plate maker's apprentice, mentioned above. He was only a boy, and his case might, one would think, have been treated more leniently. Another of the victims was a man who cut his throat while delirious from a "pleuritic fever." Seven other suicides were those of prisoners in Newgate or in Poultry Compter. One of them, under sentence of death, was due to meet the hangman within the week. The condemned man had been chained to the floor of his cell so that he could not reach the window, but he managed to hang himself with his garters from an iron bolt.

A prisoner who was to be brought before the magistrates charged with theft shot himself. A servant girl cut her throat after garments and money allegedly stolen from her master's home were found in her chest. A son who shot himself had quarreled with his father when accused of stealing money from the latter. Perhaps the coroners' juries were swayed by the fact that these individuals either were prisoners or had been accused of theft.

The last two persons judged to have murdered themselves were minority members of the community.

A Spanish nobleman shot himself. He had been depressed and "temporarily deranged in his mind" because of financial troubles, the departure of friends, and other problems.

A Portuguese Jew took a fatal dose of opium. According to the depositions of his daughter, when he went to view the body of his infant son the father was very ill, complained of his head, and became speechless. An apothecary who was called thought the man might have been suffering from apoplexy and bled him, but there was no improvement. An autopsy performed by Mr. Thomas Blizard, Mr. William Blizard, and Robert Longley, apothecary, revealed a large quantity of opium in the digestive tract.[10] The brain showed no sign of disease or violence. A friend of the deceased said that the latter had been accused of the murder of another Portuguese Jew and his servant and was greatly distressed.

A document attached to this last inquisition was addressed to Thomas Shelton, the coroner, and signed by the churchwardens of the parish where the death occurred. It read:

> Agreeable to your Warrant directed to us for Burying the Body of David Mendez, in some public Highway, and likewise to make you a return of the place where the Body was Buried.
>
> This is to Certify that the Body of David Mendez was Buried about 3 o'clock on Sunday Morning last in the Highway, Bishopsgate Street, between Sun Street and Union Street.
>
> 28 Jan. 1793.

No similar record was found in connection with any other death. Whether the ritual of burial of a *felo de se* at night under a highway was observed on other occasions is not apparent.[11]

In Elizabethan times and earlier it was customary for a stake to be driven through the heart of a person who had "murdered" himself. Burial, carried out during the hours of darkness, was also under a highway. The practice had its origins in the pre-medieval worship of Hecate and in beliefs relating to crossroads and vampires. While such superstitions had faded by the end of the eighteenth century, the *felo de se* was still regarded harshly by the authorities. Not until 1823 was an act (4 George IV, c. 52) passed to amend

[9] (N. 7), p. 358.

[10] The method used to identify the opium was not explained.

[11] See n. 7.

the laws and usages relating to the interment of the remains of persons, against whom a finding of *felo de se* shall be had . . . it shall not be lawful for any coroner, or other officer having authority to hold inquests, to issue any warrant or other process directing the interment of the remains of persons, against whom a finding of *felo de se* shall be had, in any public highway; but . . . such coroner or other officer shall give directions for the private interment of the remains of such persons *felo de se*, without any stake being driven through the body of such person, in the churchyard or other burial ground of the parish.

However, the 1823 law still required burial between 9 P.M. and midnight.[12]

Now let us turn to the homicides. Under English law homicide could be justifiable, excusable, or felonious. Homicide to prevent the perpetration of an atrocious crime, as in the defense of the person against murder, or in the execution of the law, as in carrying out capital punishment, or when unavoidable in performance of a legal duty, as in the suppression of a riot, was justifiable. Homicide was excusable when there was no criminal intent and the killing was in self defense or by misadventure. Felonious homicide was divided into manslaughter, unlawful killing without expressed or implied malice, and murder,[13] killing with malice aforethought, expressed or implied. Manslaughter was a clearly recognized legal concept, defined and discussed at length by Umfreville.[14] The inquisitions prepared by Thomas Shelton seldom used the term manslaughter but did differentiate between murder and other felonious killing. Thus verdicts recognizing the latter were considered by me to be equivalent to verdicts of manslaughter.

Individuals committed to trial by the coroner's court for murder or manslaughter of course had to stand trial if they were apprehended, but it was only in the judicial court that innocence or guilt was finally established and sentence was passed on those convicted.

As in some other kinds of inquests, a coroner's jury investigating a supposed homicide occasionally reached its verdict only with difficulty and even uncertainty. The following examples at least suggest the possibility of homicide; in each of them some other verdict was recorded.

The body of a warehouseman was recovered from the Thames by men grappling for sacks of malt that had been lost. The face and nose of the victim were bruised. His employees deposed that he had been happy until, five or six weeks before his death, he had been "ill treated" while walking in some fields and had received a serious head injury. Since that time he had been depressed and sometimes delirious. Then he had received a threatening letter in the two-penny post. In recent weeks he had neglected his business. The verdict was accidental death.

TABLE 13

HOMICIDES BY METHOD AND SEX OF VICTIM

	Male	Female	Not Stated	Total
Blow	21	7		28
Not stated	16	7	2	25
Vehicle	10	6		16
Umbilical hemorrhage	9	9	2	20
Shooting	7			7
Stabbing, cutting	6	5		11
Miscellaneous assault	5			5
Suffocation	5	8		13
Strangulation	3	2		5
Drowning	2	1		3
Animal	1	1		2
Exposure, starvation	1	1		2
Ship	1			1
	87	47	4	138

A laborer was taken violently ill, with delirium and much pain. His mouth and tongue were swollen. His wife said he took poison. Efforts to give an emetic failed. The wife and others were instructed to take the man to a hospital but failed to do so. There was no autopsy. The jury's verdict was natural death.

Two women who shared a room quarreled violently. Other lodgers heard a fight and the sound of blows. The next morning one of the women was found dead. There was no autopsy, but the searchers reported that her lip was swollen and she had bruises on her legs. However, they found no indication of the cause of death. The latter was ruled accidental.

A woman and her husband quarreled. He struck her on the head, knocking her senseless to the floor. The jury decided her death was due to intoxication.

A prostitute took an intoxicated man to her room in a garret just before midnight. She said that he collapsed in his clothes on the bed and that she then went downstairs, planning to leave him for the night so that she could have her supper and return to the streets. A few minutes later the man was found lying naked and dead on the stones of the courtyard. Many witnesses were examined. The verdict was accidental death.

Homicidal death was most frequently caused by a blow or blows (table 13). Umbilical hemorrhage due to allegedly deliberate failure to tie the "navel string" or umbilical cord after birth caused the deaths of 20 newborn infants. Suffocation was another common form of infanticide. Vehicles, animals, and even a ship were the direct causes of several deaths.

Comparisons of the distribution of suicides and homicides by month (table 12) is instructive. Monthly totals for the suicides ranged from 52 to 84, with the highest numbers in February and May and the lowest in November. For the much smaller number of homicides, on the other hand, the highs were in March and July, the lows were in May and November, and the variation between months was much greater.

[12] Forbes (n. 7), pp. 165–167.

[13] Under the Infanticide Act of 1922, the killing of a newborn baby became the equivalent of manslaughter. Before that time, infanticide was regarded as murder (*Encyclopaedia Britannica* (London, 1937) **15:** p. 179).

[14] (N. 7), p. 47 *et seq.*

TABLE 14

TYPES OF HOMICIDE BY SEX OF VICTIM

	Male	Female	Unknown	Total
Nonfelonious	7	1		8
Felonious				
Manslaughter	34	14		48
Murder				
Infanticide	26	23	4	53
Other	20	9		29
	87	47	4	138

Table 14 shows the categories of homicide by numbers and sex of victims. The inquisitions use the term "justifiably killed" in all eight cases of nonfelonious homicide, although by definition some of them, summarized below, would seem rather to be "excusable." The latter type of homicide was recognized and clearly defined by Umfreville in 1761 in his instructions to coroners.[15] The following examples illustrate instances in which coroners' juries reached verdicts of nonfelonious homicide.

When one man assaulted another, striking him repeatedly with a cart whip, the victim defended himself, mortally injuring his attacker.

A housebreaker intent on burglary and rape was shot by an occupant of the house (see p. 11 for text of inquisition).

A man stole a woman's bonnet in the street. She raised the hue and cry.[16] A patrol (watchman) ordered him to stop or he would fire. The thief continued to run, and the patrol discharged his blunderbuss, killing the fleeing man. The patrol returned the bonnet to the woman.

Two drunken men fought in an alehouse. One of them, using an iron bar "to defend himself," struck the other a mortal blow.

Three privates and a sergeant of marines came ashore with two officers as a press gang. Later the marines asked a constable to protect them while they returned to their ship at Deptford. They stated that "the Sailors had risen against them," confessing that one of the privates had "pricked one of the Sailors with his Bayonet, and his Officer had cut another." A riot followed. The sailor "pricked" by a bayonet, apparently before the riot began, later died in St. Thomas's Hospital of a puncture wound of the abdomen.

A ship's apprentice sleeping in the forecastle of his vessel was awakened by the rattling of the box nearby in which he kept his valuables. A thief was breaking it open. The boy spoke to a second apprentice in the next bed, who called out. The thief threatened to throttle him if he made a noise. The second boy, who had a cutlass in his bed, drew it and struck. The thief ran but in a moment fell dead.

[15] (N. 7), p. 79.

[16] A loud shouting during the pursuit of an escaping felon; all who heard were supposed to join in the outcry.

A thief shot while breaking into a house died later in Newgate (see p. 33).

An intoxicated woman tried to force her way up some stairs and into a home. The housewife pushed the intruder, who fell against a brick wall and received a fatal head injury.

Thomas Shelton used the term manslaughter in only four inquisitions. In forty others he spoke of a victim being "feloniously assaulted" or "feloniously killed" or "feloniously slain." In eight additional cases the inquisition was either blank or missing, as were the depositions, and the scanty information available was limited to endorsements, notes of a clerk, etc. However, the context made it clear that these cases involved felonious killings. Because felonies were involved, the deodands and their owners, if known, were named and the value of each deodand was stated.

Thirteen instances of manslaughter involved road accidents.

The intoxicated driver of a two-horse brewery dray ran down a child but did not stop. A witness noted the number of the dray and the brewer's name. The wagon and horses were valued at £40.

A rapidly driven ("ten miles an hour") chaise knocked a man down.

A cart pulled by a galloping horse forced a man into the path of a four-horse wagon. The hind wheel of the latter ran him down. The driver of the cart was judged guilty of felonious assault. The wheel of the wagon was valued at 5*s*.; the cart and horse, at £10.

An unknown person driving a bullock in the Islington Road teased and worried the animal. It gored a woman, who later died in hospital. The driver was accused of manslaughter. The deodand, payable by the bullock's owner, was 10*s*.

The steam vessel *Brocklebank* ran down a skiff on the Thames. An occupant of the skiff died. A man on the ship, presumably the captain, was held guilty of felonious assault.

Twenty cases of assault ended in manslaughter charges.

Two prisoners in the Fleet quarreled over a decision by the racquet master in a game of racquets. One man struck the other repeatedly. The victim, who did not return the blows, collapsed soon afterward and died the next morning.

Two men fought on a barge. One was pushed into the Thames and drowned.

A laborer hurled an earthenware pot at the head of an elderly woman, who died. The deceased had provoked the quarrel by herself throwing various objects.

A dealer in hams and cold meats, attacked by a dissatisfied customer, was thrown to the ground, suffering an internal hemorrhage.

The coroners' juries reached verdicts of murder in 82 inquests, including 53 cases representing infanticide (table 14). Records among the inquest papers regarding the murders of adults unfortunately were scanty, since when a coroner's jury committed an individual to trial for murder, it was the practice for the documents to be forwarded to the General Sessions. It is of interest that a man and two women run down by, respectively, a coach and two carts were held by coroners' juries to have been murdered by the drivers of these vehicles. Other murders were committed with bare hands, a gun, a pistol (used as a club), knives, a razor, boards, a hammer, a poker, and, inevitably, the familiar "sharp instrument" and "blunt instrument."

A deranged father killed this three-year-old son with a razor.

Two brothers quarreled at breakfast. One threw a knife. The resulting scalp wound was dressed at the hospital and at first seemed to do well, but fever and then erysipelas developed.

A laborer struck another man on the head with a wooden staff valued at 2*d*. The murderer "withdrew himself and fled for the same." The jury found that he "had no goods or Chattels Lands or Tenements."

Infanticide is believed by many authorities to have been common in various countries including England in past centuries. Evidence for the relative frequency and ease with which this crime was committed suggests that it must often have been successfully concealed; if so, the true incidence was considerably greater than available figures indicate. Exposure, starvation, and overlaying were common methods. Graunt reports that among 229,250 deaths listed in the *Bills of Mortality* for 1629–1636 and 1694–1703 were those of 529 infants "Overlaid and starved."[17] Not all of these deaths could have been by misadventure. Of 217 deaths by accident and violence in the Parish of St. Martin-in-the-Fields, London, in 1685–1687 and 1694–1703, 46 were those of infants who were overlaid.[18]

Infanticide has its roots not only in disregard for human life but sometimes also in poverty, ignorance, greed, and prejudice. Before the latter part of the nineteenth century, the high infant mortality rate from disease led to the expectation that many infants and children were bound to die and to relative apathy when the deaths occurred. Grinding poverty welcomed fewer mouths to feed. In the 1800's the easy availability of opium in various forms including popular soothing syrups, and social approval of their use, made the drugging of infants to keep them quiet an accepted practice. Ignorance, carelessness, and worse took their inevitable toll. The deliberate poisoning of children with less subtle substances, particularly arsenic, was by no means unknown. Membership in a burial club brought financial compensation to the parents when a child died. Foster care in "baby farms" was notoriously lethal, especially for the children of paupers. Such children had to be supported by the parish through taxes until at ages sometimes as early as five or six the youngsters could be put to work. Few mourned when the wretched children died, and many of them did.[19]

Social and legal attitudes regarding illegitimacy made it a threat to mother and child alike. Prejudice had existed for centuries. Under a vicious law of James I,[20] as Havard[21] has pointed out, when the body of an illegitimate newborn infant, previously abandoned by its mother, was found, the mother was to be sentenced to death for murder unless it could be proved that the infant was stillborn. The statute, discussed by Umfreville,[22] was not repealed until 1803. William Hunter, Scottish physician, accoucheur, and anatomist and brother of John, wrote with wisdom and sensitivity about the injustice of the law and the difficulties that could arise in determining whether a newborn child, found dead, had been alive at birth.[23] Percival discussed the issue in his *Medical Jurisprudence*.[24] Unless the father of an illegitimate child could be identified and be forced by law to take financial responsibility for his offspring, its maintenance became the obligation of the parish (see above), which consigned the mother to a dismal workhouse and often sent the infant to a foundling home or "baby farm." Here again the baby was the victim of its birth. According to Radbill, in nineteenth-century London four out of five illegitimate children died when put out to nurse.[25]

A prostitute secretly delivered her baby and at once "unlawfully and secretly put the said Female Child into the privy of a certain house there situate and did thereby endeavour to conceal the Birth." Fortunately for the mother, the jury agreed that the baby was stillborn.

In the City of London and Southwark inquests, infanticides outnumbered the murders of adults by almost two to one (table 14). As already stated, it is likely that by no means all infanticides that occurred were identified as such. For example, was it only a coincidence that on April 5, 7, and 8, 1792, three small children "fell" from windows in the adjoining parishes of St. Sepulchre and St. Bride? The deaths were ruled "accidental." The bodies of small babies could be disposed of without much difficulty. When the remains were found, they were usually in the

---

[17] P. 10.

[18] T. R. Forbes, "Sextons' Day Books for 1685–1687 and 1694–1703 from the Parish of St. Martin-in-the-Fields, London," *Yale Jour. Biol. Med.* **46** (1973): pp. 142–150.

[19] Havard, *Homicide*, pp. 52–54; S. X. Radbill, "Pediatrics," In: A. G. Debus, ed., *Medicine in the Seventeenth Century* (Berkeley, Calif, 1974), pp. 243–244; Radbill, "Child Abuse," p. 8; W. L. Langer, "Checks on Population Growth: 1750–1850," *Scient. Amer.* **226** (1972): pp. 93–99; Langer, "Infanticide: A Historical Survey," *History Childhood Quart.* **1** (1974): pp. 353–366; (N. 1), Hair; Hair, "Homicide, Infanticide, and Child Assault in Late Tudor Middlesex," *Local Pop. Studies*, No. 9 (1972): pp. 43–46; Lomax, "Opiates."

[20] 21 Jac., c. 27.

[21] Pp. 6–7.

[22] (N. 7), pp. 44–45.

[23] W. Hunter, "On the Uncertainty of the Signs of Murder in the Case of Bastard Children," *Med. Observ. Inquiries* **6** (1783): pp. 266–290. The problem will be discussed in the next chapter.

[24] Thomas Percival, *Medical Jurisprudence* (1794, no place), pp. 58–63.

[25] *Child Abuse*, p. 8.

Thames, in a privy, or simply in a box or bundle left in a street or ditch. Sometimes decomposition made it difficult or impossible to determine the cause of death. In at least 23 cases of recognized infanticide the baby appeared to have had a fatal hemorrhage due to failure to tie the umbilical cord. Other infants died from a blow, suffocation, strangulation, or exposure. In only three instances did it appear that the mother was known and in only six deaths was the murderer identified. Seven babies were of unspecified age, six were from a few days to one month old, and the remainder were thought to be newborn. Often the body was examined by a surgeon, or sometimes an apothecary or doctor of physic, and occasionally an autopsy was performed (see next chapter).

A woman, not the mother, "who had the care and charge of the said child to nurse did not supply it with suff. food . . . that it had not suff. covers was permitted to lay in a Drawer upon a pillow or cape in its filth." The nurse was charged with murder.

A laborer found the body of a baby boy while cleaning a drain leading from the "necessary" of The Bell, an inn.

The corpse of a baby girl who had been strangled was discovered "in a hole of Dr. Hunter's meeting house at London Wall."

A tiny corpse wrapped in a handkerchief was found in the street where the infant had been left "exposed to the inclemency of the weather with the view and intent, and for the purpose of effecting the death of the said new born Male Child."

In at least half a dozen other cases the circumstances as reported strongly suggest infanticide but the jury decided either that death was accidental or that, in one case, the baby was premature.

A woman said that she had only two labor pains, called in vain for help, delivered her baby while standing, then fainted. The baby died of a hemorrhage.

Another woman also reported that her child was born while she was standing. She ascribed the baby's severe head injury to its having fallen to the floor.

A premature infant, found alive in a privy, died an hour or two later. A surgeon said the baby was in about its sixth month and would not have survived anyway.

A word should be added regarding stillbirths. As indicated in table 2, only 40 of them came to inquest. The actual number during this period must have been much greater, but apparently an inquest was not required for such stillborn deaths as were reported unless the circumstances were suspicious. Umfreville is not enlightening on this point. An inquisition with a verdict of stillbirth read in part as follows:

> one Jenny Herbert being pregnant and with child . . . it so happened that said child while it was ensient[26] and unborn and in the womb of the said Jenny Herbert by the act of providence and by no violent means or method whatsoever did die. . . .

[26] *Enceinte*, unborn. Note that here term refers to the child, not the mother.

VII. THE MEDICAL MAN AND THE INQUEST

Prior to the nineteenth century, perhaps the most serious deficiency in operation of the inquest had been the failure, for various reasons, to elicit adequate, regular medical testimony. England had lagged literally centuries behind the Continent in the developing field of forensic medicine.[1] Umfreville's guide for coroners, published in 1761, was primarily a legal work but it did advise[2] that

> If the Inquiry be of the Death of one Man by another, and it be doubtful, whether the Wound be mortal or not, you ought to have a Surgeon, to be present and attend with you, to examine and shew the Wound; and who should likewise attend the Coroner and give his Evidence upon Oath.
>
> If the Parish Surgeon shall refuse to attend without being paid (and this I have known objected) you may then direct your Warrant to the Church Wardens and Overseers of the Parish where the Inquest is taking, to procure and send one.

Umfreville's "Form of a *Summons* for the Assistance of a Surgeon" stated that the surgeon should be ordered "to open and inspect the Body"[3] and "to give Evidence and be examined on his Majesty's Behalf" at the inquest.[4]

On the Continent, postmortem examinations were being performed almost routinely by the seventeenth century. The next hundred years saw further development of the autopsy as a method of investigation.[5] Evidence is scanty as to when British surgeons began with any regularity to perform postmortem examinations in order to obtain information for presentation at inquests. However, current research by the author is producing some information. Depositions from a series of 377 inquests, mostly on homicides, in London and Middlesex between 1673 and 1782 include the reports of postmortem examination of 109 of the bodies. As in the present series of inquest records, there is no mention of histological observations; the microscopic study of human tissues was not to come into its own until almost the middle of the nineteenth century.[6]

We have evidence that in England in the second half of the eighteenth century Percivall Pott,[7] William

[1] Havard, *Homicide*, pp. 1, 2, 8; E. H. Ackerknecht, "Legal Medicine in Transition (16th–18th centuries)," *Ciba Symp.* **11** (1950): pp. 1291–1298. Forensic medicine was not taught in a British university until 1821.

[2] *Lex coronatoria*, pp. 295–296.

[3] Quite often, only the exterior of a body was examined for injuries and other signs that might suggest the cause of death. I have not classified such a procedure as an autopsy unless in addition the body was opened and internal structures were observed. The terms *autopsy* and *postmortem*, incidentally, do not occur in this series of inquest records, nor does Umfreville (n. 2) use them.

[4] (N. 2), p. 510.

[5] Radbill, "Pediatrics," p. 254; L. S. King and M. C. Meehan, "A History of the Autopsy," *Amer. Jour. Path.* **73** (1973): pp. 514–544.

[6] (N. 5), King and Meehan; G. W. Corner, *Anatomy* (New York, 1930), p. 41; T. R. Forbes, "Inquests into London and Middlesex Homicides," *Yale Jour. Biol. Med.* **50** (1977): pp. 207–220.

[7] T. R. Forbes, "Percivall Pott Performs a Postmortem," *Bull. N.Y. Acad. Med.*, second ser., **51** (1975): pp. 272–276.

Hunter,[8] John Hunter,[9] and Astley Cooper,[10] all of them renowned surgeon-anatomists, were concerning themselves with the medicolegal importance of careful postmortem examinations and of accurate medical testimony at inquests. The redoubtable John Hunter was called in March, 1781, to testify at the trial of John Donellan, accused of the willful murder by poison of Sir Theodosius Edward Allesley Boughton. In court three physicians and a surgeon agreed that drinking laurel water caused Boughton's death. Hunter heard the evidence but refused to support their opinion, saying that apoplexy would cause similar symptoms. He objected vigorously to the incomplete autopsy, done following exhumation ten days after the victim died. As a scientist, Hunter pointed repeatedly to the lack of solid evidence and refused to give a decision on the cause of death. The judge, summing up, referred to the firm opinions of the other medical witnesses and to Hunter's doubts. Donellan was found guilty and was hanged.[11]

Seven years after this disturbing case, Samuel Farr's *Medical Jurisprudence*, the first book in English devoted to the subject, was published.[12] It was an abridged translation of *Elementa medicinae forensis* by J. F. Faselius.[13] Farr's chapter "On Homicide" advises that[14]

> The examination of the dead body should be as soon as possible after death, in the day time, at a proper place, where a dissection, if necessary, (and it is almost always necessary) may be performed, and not according to vulgar custom, where it is found, let it be ever so improper, and likewise by proper instruments, such as are generally used by surgeons in their dissections, and not by coarse and rude knives and scissors, which may mangle and tear the body, but cannot ascertain the cause of its death.

Five other works on medical jurisprudence by British and Irish authors had appeared by 1819. Three of them[15] were of relatively little value. Thomas Percival's *Medical Jurisprudence*, in later editions called *Medical Ethics*, was largely concerned with the latter subject. However, it did include a good deal of medicolegal information that must have been of assistance to doctors of the time. Percival pointed out[16] that in cases of sudden death

> the attendance of a physician or surgeon may often be required, who should be qualified to give testimony consonant to legal, as well as to professional knowledge. To this end, he must not only be acquainted with the signs of natural death, but also of those which occur, when it is produced by accident or violence.[17]

George E. Male's *An Epitome of Juridical or Forensic Medicine; for the use of medical men, coroners, and barristers*, published in 1816,[18] was the first original book in English in this field. Male's volume, a solid, specific, and detailed presentation with many references to the medical literature, included, for example, a large section on poisons that described fatal doses, symptoms, speed of action, remedies, tests for recognition of the toxic agent, and signs to look for at autopsy. Two years later a second edition was published.[19] Soon other substantial volumes appeared,[20] no doubt inspired by Male's careful work.

In 1836 were passed both the Births and Deaths Registration Act and an act that encouraged the medicolegal investigation of accidental and violent deaths by making provision for payment for autopsies, toxicological analyses, and medical witnesses at inquests. This legislation, an *Act for the Attendance and Remuneration of Medical Witnesses at Coroners' Inquests*,[21] also authorized the coroner to require both the attendance of a medical practitioner at an inquest and, if so desired, his conduct of an autopsy. The jury, if dissatisfied with the practitioner's evidence, could oblige the coroner to call a second medical man who could be directed, if necessary, to perform a second autopsy.

A result of the act was that cases of sudden death were reported to coroners much more frequently.[22] In 1837 an additional act[23] made it legally possible for coroners to be compensated for the reasonable expenses of inquests.[24] Three years later the first medically qualified coroner was appointed. He was Thomas Wakley, founder and first editor of the *Lancet* and member of Parliament for Finsbury; he became coroner for Middlesex and a vigorous champion of reform of the coronership.[25] The justices of the peace, who were continuing to make problems for the coroners, reacted predictably to Wakley's appointment: "It is not in one case out of twenty that any medical skill is required, the cause of death being of itself sufficiently obvious."[26] The struggle for a sound

[8] W. Hunter, "Signs of Murder."

[9] T. R. Forbes, "New Manuscripts."

[10] Cooper was primarily responsible for encouraging the performance of regular and frequent postmortems at Guy's Hospital (E. R. Long, *A History of Pathology* (Baltimore, 1928), pp. 156–157).

[11] J. Dobson, *John Hunter* (1969, Edinburgh), pp. 220–222. B. T. Davis, "George Edward Male, M.D.—The Father of English Medical Jurisprudence," *Proc. Roy. Soc. Med.* **67** (1974): pp. 117–120.

[12] *Elements of medical jurisprudence. In*: T. Cooper, *Tracts on Medical Jurisprudence* (Philadelphia, 1819; first published 1788), pp. 111–280.

[13] (Geneva, 1767).

[14] (N. 12), p. 43.

[15] W. Dease, *Remarks on Medical Jurisprudence* (first published 1793) in T. Cooper (N. 11), pp. 81–110. J. Haslam, *Medical Jurisprudence, as it Relates to Insanity* in T. Cooper (n. 11), pp. 281–354. O. W. Bartley, *A Treatise on Forensic Medicine* (Bristol, 1815).

[16] P. 50.

[17] Opening of all the body cavities during a medicolegal autopsy did not become obligatory in England until 1953 (n. 1, Havard, p. 14).

[18] (London).

[19] (N. 11), Davis, G. E. Male, *Elements of Juridical or Forensic Medicine* (London, 1818).

[20] J. G. Smith, *The Principles of Forensic Medicine* (London, 1821). J. A. Paris and J. Fonblanque, *Medical Jurisprudence* (London, 1823).

[21] 6 and 7 Will. IV, c. 89.

[22] Brodrick, *Death Certification*, p. 113. Havard (n. 1), pp. 37, 44.

[23] 1 Vict., c. 68.

[24] Brodrick (n. 22), p. 113.

[25] G. Thurston, "A Queer Sort of Thing," *Med.-Legal Jour.* **37** (1969): pp. 165–171.

[26] W. R. H. Heddy, "Some Historic Inquests," *Med.-Legal Jour.* **20** (1952): pp. 122–132. (N. 1), Havard, p. 50.

TABLE 15

ANNUAL TOTALS OF INQUESTS AND OF AUTOPSIES REPORTED AT INQUESTS

Year	Inquests	Autopsies	Year	Inquests	Autopsies
1788	89	1	1811	175	8
1789	185	1	1812	136	8
1790	166	1	1813	135	11
1791	112	6	1814	135	7
1792	159		1815	134	10
1793	158	6	1816	166	25
1794	117	3	1817	174	19
1795	109		1818	217	33
1796	120	2	1819	190	15
1797	102	4	1820	175	22
1798	113	4	1821	200	30
1799	150		1822	170	27
1801	126	3	1823	216	47
1802	109	8	1824	193	34
1803	122	3	1825	200	38
1804	123	6	1826	207	37
1805	120	2	1827	213	51
1806	137	6	1828	235	46
1807	147	4	1829	193	38
1808	123	3		——	——
1809	139	4			
1810	161	8	Total	6351	581

and effective system for the medicolegal investigation of accidental and violent deaths was to continue in England throughout the nineteenth and well into the twentieth century.[27]

Table 15 makes possible a comparison of the annual numbers of inquests and of autopsies reported at these inquests in the City of London and Southwark. Of the 581 autopsies, 304 were in connection with accidental deaths of males, 100 in deaths of males from illness, 62 in deaths of females from illness, and 39 in accidental deaths of females. One notes the conspicuous increase in postmortems from 1816 on, a phenomenon no doubt inspired largely by the writings of William Hunter, Percival, Male, and others and by medicine's burgeoning interest in dissection of the human body. Table 5 reminds us that it was also at about this time that the numbers of inquests conducted in hospitals on the deaths of hospital patients showed a sharp increase.

The frequency of medical testimony at inquests on matters other than the postmortem examination also increased over the years until by the 1820's medical evidence was being presented at nearly all inquests except those in which the cause of death, for example, drowning or fall from a great height, was obvious and unquestionable.

During the eighteenth century most of the autopsies later reported on at inquests were performed by surgeons. However, as increasing numbers of sick and injured persons were admitted to hospitals and died there (table 5), more and more of the postmortems were carried out by "dressers," senior medical students. It was also the latter who with increasing frequency testified at inquests as to the appearance and condition of the deceased when admitted as a patient and as to his subsequent history in the hospital.

A dresser at St. Thomas's Hospital deposed that "this afternoon he opened the body of the deced and found two large blood Vessels ruptured one in the Thorax and the other in the Abdomen and his Liver was very much lacerated, which injuries this Dept [deponent] is of opinion occasioned the deceds death."

A dresser at Guy's Hospital "exd. [examined] the body and found the Spleen ruptured, which was the cause of his death."

Postmortem examinations reported at inquests were infrequently conducted by apothecaries, in 1816–1818 by "an Inspector of Bodies at Guy's Hospital," and at least once by a doctor of physic.

Regarding a man who cut his throat while delirious and survived for several days, an apothecary at St. Bartholomew's Hospital deposed: "Since his death his body has been opened when Dept observed three ulcers in his intestines about the size of a sixpence each. The Brain and other parts of the body of the deced were in a natural state. Dept is of opinion the death of the deced was occasioned by the diseased state of his body connected with Fever, and not from any hurt on his throat."

An apothecary examined the remains of an unidentified woman. He "opened her body and on xaming [examining] the Heart he discovered a considerable quantity of coagulated blood in the pericardium which was occd. [occasioned] by the rupture of a blood vessel."

Thomas Callaway, Inspector of Morbid Anatomy at Guy's Hospital, made a postmortem examination of the body of a man who fell from a ladder. The Inspector found four broken ribs, bruises, and "inflammation of the Membrane of the chest."

In the body of the victim of another fall, Callaway observed that the "vertebrae of his Neck was [*sic*] fractured and the spinal marrow divided."

Infrequently, a postmortem was ordered by the coroner after the inquest had begun.

On September 1, 1826, an aged, infirm man who was crossing a street was struck by the shaft of a cart or by the cart horse and received "superficial" head wounds. He died on September 7. The inquest was begun on September 9 but was continued to September 11 so that an autopsy could be performed. The surgeon reported that "there did not appear to be any violence done" within the abdomen or thorax even though the sixth and seventh ribs were fractured. The pleural cavity and lungs were filled with mucus. Death was ascribed to natural causes.

Some autopsies, at least as judged by laymen's

[27] The continuing battle for reform produced an extensive literature. For two early examples, see George Lowther, "A Knowledge of Medicine an Essential Requirement in a Coroner," *Lancet* 1 (1839): pp. 578–580; Hy. Letheby, *Report to the Honorable Commissioners of Sewers of the City of London on certain imperfect mortality returns, relating to the verdicts of coroners' juries* (1856, London).

written summaries of the medical depositions, were something less than complete, even by the standards of the time. If, for example, a head injury was suspected, only the head might be opened, the thoracic and abdominal contents being ignored. In other cases it was evident that the individual performing the autopsy was perceptive and thorough.

An emaciated male body showed no marks of violence but did reveal "oscification of the coronary artery." Verdict: natural death.

A servant girl was seen to be intoxicated in the Fleet Market on a Saturday night. The next morning she appeared to be well but said her mistress had given her "a ferocious slap on the face when she went home the overnight," i.e., the previous evening. A witness confirmed that there had been a noisy quarrel about 1 A.M. Sunday. The servant was seen at various times that day by other witnesses who thought she looked well and in good spirits. However, at about 3 P.M. she suddenly collapsed and two hours later had a convulsion. A surgeon was called at 6 P.M. He arrived promptly but found the servant had expired. Postmortem examination disclosed discoloration around the right eye and "a quantity of coagulated blood under the Dura mater which extended into the substance of the right hemisphere of the Brain . . . the right and left lateral sinuses were ruptured . . . Says that in Appoplexy there is seldom more than one extravasation met with and that not in the part of the lateral sinuses which from its form is seldom known to give way unless some considerable degree of force is used, and therefore Dept thinks the injuries which he discovered in the head of the deced were not produced by Appoplexy, but from a fall or blow or both or from passion or Fright." Verdict: natural death from apoplexy.[28]

A surgeon suspected that a woman had died of poison because her body was swollen. At autopsy the intestines appeared normal but one side of the stomach was "a little inflamed" and in the stomach wall was discovered an almost circular hole. The small amount of gastric fluid was "not at all corrosive." The surgeon was sure that death was due to the hole but had no idea what caused it. Another witness said the deceased had drunk a glass of brandy, became ill, and felt "a violent pain in the pit of her stomach for several hours before she died." Verdict: natural death.

An adult male "not being of sound mind memory and understanding but lunatic and distracted" was found in the street by a watchman. The victim was very ill and in great pain. A bystander found a paper bearing the words "oxalic acid poison." The sick man confirmed that he had swallowed nearly an ounce of the substance. He was admitted to St. Bartholomew's Hospital. Efforts to administer an emetic were unsuccessful and he died in a few minutes. Postmortem examination showed partial destruction of the esophagus and thinning by corrosion of the stomach wall. Analysis of the gastric contents revealed oxalic acid. "The head was also examined and the appearances of the brain deviated very much from a healthy appearance. I am unable to say from those appearances whether the mind was diseased but appearances not so strongly marked have been found where great aberration of mind has been known to exist."

Some of London's leading doctors appeared as expert witnesses at inquests. In addition to Percivall Pott, the Hunter brothers, and Sir Astley Cooper, the surgeons Sir William Blizard, William Cruikshank, Henry Cline, Thomas Joseph Pettigrew, and Robley Dunglison and the physicians William Charles Wells and John C. Lettsom all testified at one time or another. Lettsom, it will be recalled, attended Lord George Gordon in his last illness.

William Cruikshank[29] performed an autopsy on an attorney whose illness and death had been ascribed to apoplexy. The postmortem findings confirmed the diagnosis. The case seems unremarkable except for a written statement by Luke Hodgson of Cow Lane, a surgeon called to see the patient, in which Hodgson says that "he was satisfied of the disease, and the irrecoverable situation he [the attorney] was in. That he gave very little heed to the idle stories of the wife of the said" attorney. Unfortunately there is no further information about the stories. Hodgson, who was also surgeon to the Giltspur Street Compter, was obliged in this case to send the coroner a written deposition rather than appearing at the inquest because, as a covering letter explains, Hodgson was "engaged with a Lady in a *particular situation*; which prevents his attendance agreeable to the summons." Evidently his practice included what later became known as obstetrics. Hodgson's name appears as deponent in a number of inquests on prisoners because he was also a prison surgeon.

As pointed out in Chapter VI, infanticide was an all too common crime. It could be managed quite simply by a married parent. If an unmarried girl sought to avoid all the serious difficulties that arose with illegitimacy, she tried to conceal first her pregnancy and then the delivery and finally to dispose of the baby. Undoubtedly she sometimes succeeded and a small body would be found drifting on the Thames or a live infant, never to be identified, would be heard crying in the gutter or even in a privy. Inquests on the bodies of newborn babies were not unusual. Depositions in these cases make clear how easily the relentless finger of suspicion could fall on an unmarried servant girl or shop girl. At the inquest her master or mistress and fellow employees were questioned as to whether they had thought the girl

[28] This seems to have been a case of a fatal subdural hemorrhage. Presumably the verdict of the coroner's jury represented an effort to avoid subjecting the girl's mistress to a charge of homicide.

[29] William Cumberland Cruikshank (1745–1800), F. R. S., anatomist, was first assistant to, and later partner of, William Hunter in the Great Windmill Street school of anatomy.

might be pregnant. Had she seemed unwell? Did a search of her personal effects disclose any baby clothes? Their absence would be taken as an indication that the mother did not intend to keep her child. Did the girl's room or bedclothes show any signs of childbirth? For the wretched victim suspected both of unmarried motherhood and of infant murder there was little sympathy.

Often the putative mother was examined by a midwife or doctor for indications of a recent pregnancy. An autopsy was performed on the baby to look for signs of violence or neglect, the latter most often represented by a failure to tie the severed umbilical cord. It was also usual to remove the lungs and place them in water to see whether they would float. The theory was that, if they did so, it was by virtue of air inspired after birth and that therefore the baby had been born alive. If the lungs sank, this was usually taken as evidence of a stillbirth. The doctor also looked carefully at the lungs to determine whether they seemed to contain air.

An unmarried servant girl gave birth secretly. The body of her baby was found in a cellar. At the autopsy no marks of violence were discovered. Upon removal, the lungs floated in water, inducing the surgeon to believe they had been inflated. Nevertheless, he could not decide whether the infant was alive at birth. The jury's verdict was that the child was stillborn.

The body of a baby was found floating in a basket on the Thames. A surgeon deposed that the infant was two to three weeks old and that it had a fracture on the right side of the head which had caused death. Verdict: murder by a person or persons unknown.

A newborn baby found wrapped in a piece of calico appeared to have suffocated. The autopsy surgeon "did not discover anything which was the cause of its death; the lungs of the Child being put in water swam and from appearance of them dept believes that Child was respired. It might have breathed in its birth, and yet have died of natural causes." Verdict: murder.

An inquisition charged murder of an infant by failure "to secure and fasten the navel cord" so that the baby bled to death. The surgeon "by his opening the Child and examining its lungs . . . thinks the Child born alive. There was no appearance of violence upon the Child."

A dead newborn girl was found naked in the gutter. At autopsy the viscera appeared healthy. The lungs floated. The examiner observed that the infant "might have respired at the time of its birth, and died immediately afterward, which is sometimes the case." The ventricles of the brain contained a little "more serum than usual." There were possible signs of strangulation on the neck. An afterbirth was found in the suspect's house, and a constable shrewdly pointed out that the torn end of its umbilical cord matched the end still attached to the baby. The surgeon examined the suspected mother and found no signs of lactation. The verdict of the coroner's jury was murder.

Although the origin of the "hydrostatic test" for the lungs has been ascribed to Galen, it appears that his contribution was simply to point out that at birth the substance of the lungs, which up to then was red, heavy, and dense, is transformed by respiration to a pink, light, and thin condition. According to Brittain, Sonnenkalb in Saxony suggested the hydrostatic test in 1561.[30] In 1626 van Spieghel[31] confirmed Galen's observation, and William Harvey two years later[32] commented on the necessity for the newly delivered child to breathe as soon as its membranes are ruptured.

> How commeth it to pass, that the Foetus being now borne, and continuing yet covered over with his entire membranes, and abiding still in his water, can subsist for some hours space, without any danger of suffocation: and yet being shifted out of those membranes, if he have but once attracted the Aire into his Lungs, he cannot afterward live a minute without it, but dyeth instantly?

Johann Swammerdam in his doctoral thesis in 1667 had noted that in a fetus just before birth "the lungs are compacted on themselves and the chest is expanded, without any denser air inside between the lungs and ribs."[33] Swammerdam's contemporary, the Danish anatomist Thomas Bartholin,[34] observed that

> The Substance [of the lung] in a Child in the Womb is compact and thick; so that being cast into Water it sinks, which the Lungs of grown persons will not do.

The hydrostatic test is said to have been employed in 1682 by Dr. Johann Schreyer, a physician of Zietz, in Saxony, who two years later presented his findings in court.[35] In 1761 both Haller[36] and Morgagni[37] described the experiment in which the fetal lung sinks when placed in water while the lung which has received an inspiration does not. Morgagni, however, like many of his successors,[38] pointed out

---

[30] Cl. Galen, *De usu partium*, lib. XV, cap. VI, col. 767; R. P. Brittain, "The Hydrostatic and Similar Tests of Live Birth: A Historical Review," *Med.-Legal Jour.* **31** (1963): pp. 187–194.

[31] A. van Spieghel, *De formato foetu* (Padua, 1626), cap. 5, pp. 49–50.

[32] W. Harvey, *Anatomical Exercitations* (London, 1653; first published 1628), p. 483.

[33] J. Swammerdam, *Tractatus physico-anatomico-medicus de respiratione* (Leyden, 1667), sect. I, cap. III, p. 25.

[34] T. Bartholin, *Anatomy* (London, 1663), book II, chap. IX, p. 117.

[35] J. Nemec, *International Bibliography of the History of Legal Medicine* (Bethesda, Md., 1974), p. 19; Ackerknecht, "Early History," pp. 1295–1296. The history of the test is reviewed at length by Brittain (n. 30).

[36] A. von Haller, *Elementa physiologiae* (Lausanne, 1761) **3**, lib. 7, sect. 4, xxiv, pp. 278–280.

[37] J. B. Morgagni, *The Seats and Causes of Diseases* (New York, 1960) **1**: letter 19, pp. 536–537.

[38] (N. 8); (n. 12), p. 34; (n. 16), p. 64. J. B. Beck, *An Inaugural Dissertation on Infanticide* (New York, 1817), p. 50 *et seq.*; J. J. Elwell, *A Medico-legal Treatise on Malpractice* (New York, 1860), pp. 556–558; W. B. Woodman and C. M. Tidy, *Forensic Medicine and Toxicology* (Philadelphia, 1877), pp. 683–684; A. S. Taylor,

various circumstances in which the test would give false results. For instance, if decomposition were advanced, gas produced in the lungs of a stillborn baby might cause them to float. Modern forensic pathologists appear skeptical of the hydrostatic test.[39]

Medicine was on occasion involved with coroners and inquests in an additional and curious way, through the anatomist. The necessity for dissection of the human body as an essential part of the training of the doctor had been recognized since at least the sixteenth century. Enough cadavers were at first obtained for the anatomist and his students through legal channels, the law specifying that each year the bodies of several executed criminals be released for dissection.[40] Evidence that this procedure was still in effect at the end of the eighteenth century derives from the records of trials in 1795 and 1796.

A coroner's jury found that Matthew Dunn had murdered Thomas Price by shooting him with a carbine. At Dunn's trial he was sentenced to be hanged "and his Body afterwards dissected and anatomized pursuant to the statute in such case made and provided," the dissection to take place at the Hall of the Surgeons' Company.

At an inquest on the body of a man who had been stabbed, two of his assailants were charged with murder. Later they were sentenced to be hanged and afterward "anatomized," also at Surgeons' Hall.[41]

Edward Umfreville had included a cautionary note about such matters.[42] After presenting the suggested wording for an inquisition in cases in which a woman died after childbirth, he warned

> Surgeons who read Lectures in Midwifery, or otherwise, who, I fear, for the Sake of Experiment, (however otherwise to be approved) make it too common a Practice to operate upon dead Bodies without Leave or Authority.

It seems that a pregnant woman whose husband was absent on a ship lodged with a "Surgeon and Man-midwife" and was delivered by him. The baby died soon after birth and the mother three days later. She had no relatives in London. The surgeon opened the abdomen, lectured and demonstrated to his pupils in midwifery, and sewed the body up. When the relatives arrived to attend the funeral, they discovered the dissection

> and not knowing the true Cause, made Complaint to a Justice of the Peace, which introduced the Coroner, and the Fact was inquired into, and found as above; but the Coroner, though he approved the Use and Design in the general, yet censured the Act as practised upon private Property, without License.

By the latter part of the eighteenth century the demand for bodies for dissection in London had grown until the legal supply was no longer adequate. The inevitable result was the illegal procurement of cadavers through grave robbing or worse.[43] On occasion, a body obtained in one city was shipped by professional grave robbers in a barrel, box, or other container to London, where a buyer was waiting. Sometimes the shipment did not reach its destination. When the gruesome remains were discovered, an inquest of course had to be held.[44]

The bookkeeper at the Cross Keys Inn in Wood Street deposed that one morning a hamper and a package wrapped in matting were delivered to the inn by the Chatham Coach. The two shipments were addressed to individuals in Oxford Street and Old Street "and both of them directed to be left till called for. The Hamper which was directed for Oxford Street was taken there, but no person being found to answer the address it was bro't back, and a suspicion arising the Hamper was opened and it was found to contain the dead body of a female, and afterwards the matting was opened and in that was the dead body of a man. That yesterday morning a man came for the Hamper and matting and produced two directions corresponding with their directions and then he paid for the Carriage and afterward was taken into custody." A surgeon who examined the bodies found no marks of violence and asserted that the two individuals died natural deaths. The jury agreed.

Perhaps so. But smothering need not leave any obvious sign. And why select this definitely unorthodox method of transportation and use a false address?

After the Hull steam packet arrived in the Thames, suspicion fell on a broken box that had been brought on deck to be loaded into a lighter. The mate opened the container and found the decomposed body of a girl aged 18 to 20. The hair had been cut off. The case was addressed to a surgical instrument maker in Giltspur Street but no one knew who had made the shipment. A wharfinger at Custom House Quay found "no

A Manual of Medical Jurisprudence (Philadelphia, 1892), pp. 538–539. See also S. Smith, "The History and Development of Forensic Medicine," *Brit. Med. Jour.* **1** (1951): pp. 599–607.

[39] (N. 1), Havard, p. 7; F. E. Camps, ed., *Gradwohl's Legal Medicine* (Baltimore, 1968), p. 443; K. Simpson, *Forensic Medicine* (London, 1969), pp. 162–163; C. J. Polson and D. J. McGee, *Essentials of Forensic Medicine* (Oxford, 1973), pp. 538–539; E. Rentoul and H. Smith, eds., *Glaister's Medical Jurisprudence and Toxicology* (Edinburgh, 1973), pp. 404–405.

[40] T. R. Forbes, "A Note on the Procurement of Bodies for Dissection at the Royal College of Physicians of London in 1694 and 1710," *Jour. Hist. Med. Allied Sci.*, **29** (1974): pp. 332–334.

[41] "London Session Book," Sept., 1793, to Feb., 1797 (Corporation of London Records Office).

[42] Pp. 474–476.

[43] Professional criminals murdered men and women, usually by smothering, to obtain bodies. The victims were in most cases derelicts, prostitutes, and others not likely to be missed. The most notorious offenders were William Burke and William Hare, brought to trial in 1828 in Edinburgh for a series of sixteen murders, all performed to procure bodies for dissection. The public outcry at the trial helped to lead to passage in 1832 of the Warburton Act, a law which greatly reduced the illegal procurement of bodies and the related abuses. See, for example, A. F. Guttmacher, "Bootlegging Bodies; A History of Body-snatching," *Bull. Soc. Med. Hist. Chicago* **4** (1935): pp. 353–402.

[44] All of the following inquests took place between 1819 and 1829, when grave robbing was at its height in England.

appearance of violence." The jury did not reach a verdict.

A box sent by the Leeds coach to a nonexistent London address ended in a warehouse. In the box was the body of a baby girl. Verdict: natural causes.

A freight basket was delivered by coach to the Crow and Falcon Inn. When after several days it had not been called for, the basket was opened and found to contain the decomposed body of a child. There were no signs of injury. The verdict was open.

The captain of a steamship deposed that while it was at its quay in Limerick, Ireland, a stranger in a coach gave the captain a cask for delivery at an address in London. The bill of lading described the contents as pigs' legs. An excise officer on duty at the wharf in London removed the head of the cask, uncovering the bodies of a woman and child. The cause of death was not discovered, and the coroner's jury did not reach a verdict.

Of course we have no direct proof that any of these bodies were intended for the anatomist. But all the evidence points that way, and it is difficult to imagine any other reason for the transportation of bodies in the manner described. Grave robbing was a peculiar crime, growing partly from necessity in a day when there was no legal provision for an adequate supply of material for dissection and partly from greed. It is one misdeed, at least, that seems long since to have disappeared.

BIBLIOGRAPHY

ACKERKNECHT, E. H. 1950. "Legal Medicine in Transition (16th–18th Centuries)." *Ciba Symp.* **11:** pp. 1291–1298.

ANGUS, J. 1854. "Old and New Bills of Mortality; Movement of the Population; Deaths and Fatal Diseases in London During the Last Fourteen Years." *Jour. Statist. Soc. London* **17:** pp. 117–142.

BABINGTON, A. 1971. *The English Bastille* (London, MacDonald).

BAILEY, F. A. 1934. "Coroners' Inquests Held in the Manor of Prescot, 1746–89." *Trans. Hist. Soc. Lancashire and Cheshire* **86:** pp. 21–39.

BARTHOLIN, T. 1663. *Anatomy* (London, Peter Cole).

BARTLEY, O. W. 1815. *A Treatise on Forensic Medicine; or Medical Jurisprudence* (Bristol, Barry).

BECK, J. B. 1817. *An Inaugural Dissertation on Infanticide* (New York, J. Seymour).

[BIRCH, T., ed.] 1759. *A Collection of the Yearly Bills of Mortality* (London, A. Millar).

BRITTAIN, R. P. 1963. "The Hydrostatic and Similar Tests of Live Birth: a Historical Review." *Med.-Legal Jour.* **31:** pp. 187–194.

BRODRICK, NORMAN, *et al.* 1971. *Report of the Committee on Death Certification and Coroners* (London, Her Majesty's Stationery Office).

BUER, M. C. 1968. *Health, Wealth, and Population in the Early Days of the Industrial Revolution* (New York, Howard Fertig).

BURNETT, J. 1969. *A History of the Cost of Living* (Harmondsworth, Middlesex, Penguin).

CAMPS, F. E., ed. 1968. *Gradwohl's Legal Medicine* (Baltimore, Williams and Wilkins).

CARTWRIGHT, F. F. 1974. "Robert Bentley Todd's Contributions to Medicine." *Proc. Roy. Soc. Med.* **67:** pp. 893–897.

CASSEDY, J. H. 1973. "Introduction." In: *Mortality in Preindustrial Times; the Contemporary Verdict* (Westmead, Farnborough, Hants, Gregg International).

CLARK, D. W. "A Crane of Pepysian Times." *Country Life.* 28 Dec. [n.p.].

——— 1933. "The Harwich Crane," *Essex Review* **62:** pp. 1–15.

[Colquhoun, P.] 1798. *A Treatise on the Police of London* (Philadelphia, Benjamin Davies).

——— 1800. *A Treatise on the Commerce and Police of the River Thames* (London, Joseph Mawman).

COOPER, T., ed. 1819. *Tracts on Medical Jurisprudence* (Philadelphia, James Webster).

CORNER, G. W. 1930. *Anatomy* (New York, Hoeber).

CREIGHTON, C. 1965. *A History of Epidemics in Britain* (London, Frank Cass).

DAVIS, B. T. 1974. "George Edward Male M.D.—the Father of English Medical Jurisprudence." *Proc. Roy. Soc. Med.* **67:** pp. 117–120.

DEASE, W. 1819. "Remarks on Medical Jurisprudence." In: T. Cooper, ed., *Tracts on Medical Jurisprudence* (Philadelphia, James Webster).

"Death by the 'Visitation of God.' " *Lancet* **1** (1874): p. 452.

DICKENS, C. 1880. *Dickens's Dictionary of London* (London, Charles Dickens).

DOBSON, J. 1969. *John Hunter* (Edinburgh, E. & S. Livingstone).

ELWELL, J. J. 1860. *A Medico-legal Treatise on Malpractice* (New York, J. S. Voorhies).

Encyclopaedia Britannica (London, 1937).

EVANS, E. P. 1906. *The Criminal Prosecution and Capital Punishment of Animals* (New York, Dutton).

FARR, S. 1819. "Elements of Medical Jurisprudence." In: T. Cooper, ed., *Tracts on Medical Jurisprudence* (Philadelphia, James Webster).

FARR, W. 1885. *Vital Statistics* (London, Sanitary Inst.).

FASEL, J. F. 1767. *Elementa medicinae forensis* (Jena, J. W. Hartung).

FITZHERBERT, A. 1545. *The New Booke of Justices of Peace* (London, Wyllyam Myddylton).

FORBES, T. R. 1971. *Chronicle from Aldgate* (New Haven, Yale University Press).

——— 1973. "Two New John Hunter Manuscripts." *Guildhall Stud. London History* **1:** pp. 24–27.

——— 1973. "Sextons' Day Books for 1685–1687 and 1694–1703 from the Parish of St. Martin-in-the-Fields, London." *Yale Jour. Biol. Med.* **46:** pp. 142–150.

——— 1973. "London Coroners' Inquests for 1590." *Jour. History Med. Allied Sci.* **28:** pp. 376–386.

——— 1974. "The Searchers." *Bull. N.Y. Acad. Med.*, second ser., **50:** pp. 1031–1038.

——— 1974. "A Note on the Procurement of Bodies for Dissection at the Royal College of Physicians of London in 1694 and 1710." *Jour. Hist. Med. Allied Sci.* **29:** pp. 332–334.

——— 1975. "Percivall Pott Performs a Postmortem." *Bull. N.Y. Acad. Med.*, second ser., **51:** pp. 272–276.

——— 1977. "Inquests into London and Middlesex Homicides, 1673–1782." *Yale Jour. Biol. Med.* **50:** pp. 207–220.

GALEN, C. *De usu partium.*

GLYNN, J. 1970. *Rudimentary Treatise on the Construction of Cranes* (Bath, Kingsmead Reprints).

GRAUNT, J. 1759. "Natural and Political Observations on the Bills of Mortality." In: [T. Birch, ed.], *A Collection of the Yearly Bills of Mortality, from 1657 to 1758 Inclusive* (London, A. Millar).

GROSS, C., ed. 1896. "Select Cases from the Coroners' Rolls A.D. 1265–1413 with a Brief Account of the Office of Coroner." *Selden Soc. Pub.* **9** (London, Bernard Quaritch).

GUTTMACHER, A. F. 1935. "Bootlegging Bodies; a History of Body-snatching." *Bull. Soc. Med. Hist. Chicago* **4:** pp. 353–402.

HAIR, P. E. H. 1969. "Accidental Death and Suicide in Shropshire, 1780–1809." *Trans. Shropshire Archaeol. Soc.* **59:** pp. 63–75.

——— 1970. "A Note on the Incidence of Tudor Suicide." *Local Pop. Studies.* **5:** pp. 36–43.

——— 1971. "Deaths from Violence in Britain: a Tentative Secular Survey." *Pop. Studies* **25:** pp. 5–24.

——— 1972. "Homicide, Infanticide, and Child Assault in Late Tudor Middlesex." *Local Pop. Studies.* **9:** pp. 43–46.

HALLER, A. 1761. *Elementa physiologiae* (Lausanne, Sigismund d'Arnay).

HARVEY, W. 1653. *Anatomical Exercitations* (London, James Young).

HASLAM, J. 1819. "Medical Jurisprudence, As It Relates to Insanity, According to the Law of England." In: T. Cooper, ed. *Tracts on Medical Jurisprudence* (Philadelphia, James Webster).

HAVARD, J. D. J. 1960. *The Detection of Secret Homicide* (London, Macmillan).

HEDDY, W. R. H. 1952. "Some Historic Inquests." *Medico-Legal Jour.* **20:** pp. 122–132.

HOGG, J. 1837. *London As It Is* (London, John Macrone).

HOWARD, J. 1780. *The State of the Prisons in England and Wales* (Warrington, William Eyres).

HUNNISETT, R. F. 1961. "Bedfordshire Coroners' Rolls." *Publ. Bedfordshire Histor. Record Soc.* **41:** pp. i–xlv, 1–165.

——— 1961. *The Medieval Coroner* (Cambridge, University Press).

HUNTER, W. 1783. "On the Uncertainty of the Signs of Murder in the Case of Bastard Children." *Med. Obs. Inq.* **6:** pp. 266–290.

HYDE, W. W. 1916. "The Prosecution and Punishment of Animals and Lifeless Things in the Middle Ages and Modern Times." *Univ. Penna. Law Rev.* **64:** pp. 696–730.

JACKSON, P. 1971. *London Bridge* (London, Cassell).

"Journal of the Common Council of the City of London." Corporation of London Records Office **71,** July 24, 1788.

KING, L. S., and M. C. MEEHAN. "A History of the Autopsy: a Review." *Amer. Jour. Pathology* **73:** pp. 514–544.

LANGBEIN, I. L. 1933. "The Jury of Presentment and the Coroner." *Columbia Law Rev.* **33:** pp. 1329–1365.

LANGER, W. L. 1972. "Checks on Population Growth: 1750–1850." *Scient. Amer.* **226:** pp. 93–99.

——— 1974. "Infanticide: a Historical Survey." *Hist. Childhood Quart.* **1:** pp. 353–366.

LETHEBY, H. 1856. *Report to the Honorable Commissioners of Sewers of the City of London on Certain Imperfect Mortality Returns, Relating to the Verdicts of Coroners' Juries* (London, M. Lownds).

LOMAX, E. 1973. "The Uses and Abuses of Opiates in Nineteenth-century England." *Bull History Med.* **47:** pp. 167–176.

London Bridge. 1971 (London, McCulloch).

"London Session Book." Corporation of London Records Office Sept. 1793 to Feb. 1797.

LONG, E. R. 1928. *A History of Pathology* (Baltimore, Williams & Wilkins).

LOWTHER, GEORGE 1839. "A Knowledge of Medicine an Essential Requisite in a Coroner." *Lancet* **1:** pp. 578–580.

MACHT, D. I. 1913. "The Ancient Office of Coroner." *Johns Hopkins Hosp. Bull.* **24:** pp. 148–153.

MALE, G. E. 1816. *Epitome of Juridical or Forensic Medicine* (London, E. Cox).

——— 1818. *Elements of Juridical or Forensic Medicine* (London, E. Cox).

MANT, A. K. 1971. "Official Medico-legal Investigation under the Coroner's System in London, England." *Med.-Legal Bull.* **20:** pp. 1–8.

MARSHALL, J. 1832. *Mortality of the Metropolis* (London, Treuttel, Würtz, and Richter).

MCCULLOCH, J. R. 1854. *A Descriptive and Statistical Account of the British Empire* (London, Longman, Brown, Green, and Longmans).

"Minutes of the Common Council of the City of London." Corporation of London Records Office, July 14, 1829.

MORGAGNI, J. B. 1960. *The Seats and Causes of Diseases*, trans. by B. Alexander (New York, Hafner).

NEMEC, J. 1974. *International Bibliography of the History of Legal Medicine* (Bethesda, Md., Dept. Health, Education and Welfare).

OAKLEY, A. F. 1971. "Reresby and the Moor." *History Med.* **3:** pp. 27–29.

PARIS, J. A., and J. Fonblanque. 1823. *Medical Jurisprudence* (London, W. Phillips).

[PERCIVAL, T.] 1794. *Medical Jurisprudence*. [no place, no pub.].

PETTY, SIR W. 1759. "Another Essay in Political Arithmetic" In: [T. Birch, ed.] *A Collection* (London, A. Millar).

PILLING, H. H. 1970. "Social Change and the Coronership." *Med., Sci. Law* **10:** pp. 238–243.

PLATT, J. C. 1844. "Bills of Mortality." In: C. Knight, ed., *London*. (London, C. Knight).

POLSON, C. J., and D. J. MCGEE. 1973. *The Essentials of Forensic Medicine* (Oxford, Pergamon).

PURCHASE, W. B., and H. W. WOLLASTON. 1957. *Jervis on the Office and Duties of Coroners* (London, Sweet & Maxwell).

RADBILL, S. X. 1968. "A History of Child Abuse and Infanticide." In: R. E. Helfer and C. H. Kempe, eds., *The Battered Child* (Chicago, Univ. Chicago Press).

——— 1974. "Pediatrics." In: A. G. Debus, ed., *Medicine in Seventeenth Century England* (Berkeley, U. Calif. Press).

REES, A. 1819. "Crane." In: *The Cyclopaedia* (London, Longman, Hurst, Rees, Orme & Brown).

Registrar General's Statistical Review of England and Wales for the Year 1972 (London, Her Majesty's Stationery Office, 1974).

RENTOUL, E., and H. SMITH, eds. 1973. *Glaister's Medical Jurisprudence and Toxicology* (Edinburgh, Churchill Livingstone).

Report of the Officers' and Clerks' Committee on the Office of Coroner of London and Southwark Presented to Common Council 6 August 1829 (London, Arthur Taylor, 1829).

ROSEN, G. 1943. *The History of Miners' Diseases* (New York, Schuman).

RUMBELOW, D. 1971. *I Spy Blue* (London, Macmillan).

SCHILLING, R. S. F. 1973. "Developments in Occupational Health." In: R. S. F. Schilling, ed., *Occupational Health Practice* (London, Butterworths).

SHAPIRO, E. D., and A. DAVIS 1972. "Law and Pathology through the Ages. The Coroner and His Descendants—Legitimate and Illegitimate." *N.Y. State Jour. Med.* **72:** pp. 805–809.

SHARPE, R. R. 1913. *Calendar of Coroners' Rolls of the City of London, A.D. 1300–1378* (London, Richard Clay).

SHEPPARD, F. 1971. *London 1808–1870: The Infernal Wen* (London, Secker & Warburg).

SHORT, T. 1750. *New Observations* (London, T. Longman and A. Millar).

SIMPSON, K. 1969. *Forensic Medicine* (London, Edward Arnold).

Sixth Annual Report of the Registrar General of Births, Deaths and Marriages in England (London, W. Clowes, 1845).

SMITH, J. G. 1821. *The Principles of Forensic Medicine* (London, T. & G. Underwood).

SMITH, R. 1961. *Sea-coal for London* (London, Longmans).

SMITH, S. 1951. "The History and Development of Forensic Medicine." *Brit. Med. Jour.* **1:** pp. 599–607.

SPIEGHEL, A. VAN DER. 1626. *De formato foetu* (Padua, I. B. de Martinis & L. Pasquato).

STEPHEN, J. F. 1883. *A History of the Criminal Law of England* (London, Macmillan).

SWAMMERDAM, J. 1667. *Tractatus physico-anatomico-medicus de respiratione*. (Leyden, Gaasbeeck).

TAYLOR, A. S. 1892. *A Manual of Medical Jurisprudence* (Philadelphia, Lea).

"Thomas Shelton, Esq." *Gentleman's Mag.* **99,** 2 (1829): p. 89.

THURSTON, G. 1969. "A Queer Sort of Thing." *Med.-Legal Jour.* **37:** pp. 165–171.

TIMBS, J. [1867]. *Curiosities of London* (London, Virtue).

UMFREVILLE, E. 1761. *Lex coronatoria* (London, R. Griffiths).

WALDO, F. J. 1911. "The Ancient Office of Coroner." *Trans. Med.-Legal Soc. London* **8:** pp. 101–133.

WALFORD, C. 1881. "On the Number of Deaths from Accident, Negligence, Violence, and Misadventure in the United Kingdom and Some Other Countries." *Jour. Statist. Soc.* **44:** pp. 444–527.

WATSON, W. N. B. 1972. "Thomas Robertson, Naval Surgeon, 1793–1828." *Bull. History Med.* **46:** pp. 131–149.

WELCH, C. 1894. *History of the Tower Bridge* (London, Smith, Elder).

WELLINGTON, R. H. 1905. *The King's Coroner* (London, W. Clowes).

WESTCOTT, W. W. 1910. "A Note upon Deodands." *Trans. Med.-Leg. Soc. London* **10:** pp. 91–97.

WILKES, J. 1810. *Encyclopaedia Londinensis* (London, J. Adlard).

WILKINSON, J. 1651. *A Treatise . . . Concerning the Office and Authorities of Coroners and Sheriffs* (London, W. Lee).

WOODMAN, W. B., and C. M. TIDY. 1877. *Forensic Medicine and Toxicology*. (Philadelphia, Lindsay & Blakiston).

INDEX

Oversize 060 Am35t v.68 pt.1

Forbes, Thomas Rogers.

Crower's quest /